AIRBUS WIDE-BODIED
JETLINERS

AIRBUS WIDE-BODIED
JETLINERS

ROBBIE SHAW

ACKNOWLEDGEMENTS

I would like to thank the press office of Airbus Industrie, who have been very helpful during the compilation of this volume. I would also like to thank my wife Eileen both for the time taken to proof read my work (which must be very difficult for someone with absolutely no interest in aviation!) and for her endless patience during my enforced absences – either in front of a word processor, or in some far-flung corner of the world with a heavy camera bag over my shoulder.

EDITOR'S NOTE

To make the Osprey Civil Aircraft series as authoritative as possible, the editor would be interested in hearing from any individual who may have relevant information relating to the aircraft/operators featured in this, or any other, volume published by Osprey Aviation. Similarly, comments on the editorial content of this book would also be most welcome. Please write to Tony Holmes at 10 Prospect Road, Sevenoaks, Kent, TN13 3UA, Great Britain.

First published in Great Britain in 1999 by Osprey Publishing,
Elms Court, Chapel Way, Botley, Oxford, OX2 9LP

ISBN 1 85532 868 2

Edited by Tony Holmes
Cutaway drawings by Mike Badrocke
Page design by Paul Kime

Origination by Valhaven Ltd, Isleworth, UK
Printed in Hong Kong

99 00 01 02 03   10 9 8 7 6 5 4 3 2 1

FRONT COVER *Toronto-based Canada 3000 was the world's premier operator of the A330-200, receiving its first aircraft (C-GGWB) on 29 April 1998. The machine is seen six months later departing Gatwick on 12 October 1998*

BACK COVER *Austrian Airlines A310-320 OE-LAD Chicago is seen at Geneva during a brief stopover on a transatlantic flight from Vienna. Built in 1991, this aircraft was the last of four A310s delivered to the Austrian flag carrier*

TITLE PAGE *Turkish airliners are a common sight at airports in north-west Germany, as they regularly transport the large immigrant and guest worker populations in the latter country to and from Turkey. Although much of this flying is carried out by charter companies, national flag carrier THY Turk Hava Yollari - Turkish Airlines also undertakes its share of the work. Here, 1988-build A310-300 TC-JCY CORUH taxies in at Dusseldorf at the end of yet another flight from Turkey in September 1998*

RIGHT *Boldly advertising the company name, underscored with Airbus Industrie 'house colours', the modified tail of the A300-600ST Super Transport bears the word SKYLINK on its starboard side*

PAGE 128 *Prototype A330-200 F-WWKA was photographed at Farnborough 98*

Contents

Right *Seen at Toronto airport just weeks after arriving in Canada on 7 May 1997, Skyservice's ex-LTU A330-300 C-FBUS proudly displays the boast First A330 in North America. There are currently just two A330 operators in North America, and both are flown by Canadian charter carriers. Formed in 1986, Skyservice operates a small number of A320s on internal charters in Canada and across the border into the USA. C-FBUS was acquired by Skyservice for employment on the company's transatlantic routes to Western Europe*

Introduction

With the September 1998 announcement by British Airways of an order for up to 188 aircraft from the A320 family, it seemed that Britain's national airline had finally woken up to a fact known by most of its competitors – Airbus Industrie airliners are at least as good, if not better than those built by Boeing.

Airbus's history can be traced back to 1965 when a joint requirement was issued by British European Airways (BEA) and Air France for a high-density short/medium range jetliner. Lufthansa also expressed an interest in such an aircraft, and on 26 September 1967 the governments from these three countries signed a Memorandum of Understanding. One proviso of this agreement was that orders for 75 aircraft had to be forthcoming before the go-ahead would be sanctioned. When such orders failed to materialise, a short-sighted British government withdrew financial support in 1969.

Fortunately for the British aerospace industry, Hawker Siddeley Aviation had more faith in the project and supplied funds independently in order to remain an active partner. Despite a lack of official government interest from Britain, France, Germany, the Netherlands and Spain fully supported the project, resulting in Airbus Industrie being formally set up in December 1970.

Along with Hawker Siddeley, the other participating manufacturers – Aerospatiale, Deutsche Airbus, Fokker-VFW and CASA – contributed the necessary capital by securing repayable loans from their respective governments. The French and German partners were the largest shareholders with 37.9 per cent each, while Hawker Siddeley, which later became British Aerospace, acquired a 20 per cent share after the British government re-negotiated admittance back into the consortium.

The two largest shareholders naturally

Monarch Airlines is the only UK-based passenger operator of the A300, flying four leased -600R variants on both high-density European as well as transatlantic charter services. Although Luton-based, Monarch operates more services out of London/Gatwick than any other airport. Built in 1989, G-MONR is the oldest -600R in the fleet, and it is seen here in March 1997 climbing out of Gatwick bound for Tenerife, in the Canary Islands, which is a popular year-round destination for British holiday-makers

accounted for the bulk of the work on what became known as the A300 – a wide-bodied airliner with a capacity for over 300 passengers, powered by two General Electric CF6 engines in underwing pods. This was the world's first civil twin-engined wide-body, and also the first wide-body certified for a two-man cockpit crew. At Airbus Industrie's Toulouse factory, Aerospatiale built the lower fuselage and nose section (including the flight deck) and the engine pylons. In Hamburg, Deutsche Airbus was tasked with constructing the centre, rear and upper fuselage and vertical tail, whilst British Aerospace at Hawarden, near Chester, designed and built the wings. Fokker-VFW supplied the moving wing surfaces such as flaps and ailerons, and responsibility for the horizontal tail surfaces was given to CASA, who also fabricated the fuselage and landing gear doors in Spain.

As Airbus Industrie was primarily a French-driven consortium, Toulouse was naturally chosen as the final assembly location for the A300, and the completed sections of aircraft were all duly flown in to the vast factory. In order to facilitate the moving of large items such as the wings and vertical tail, two Aero Spacelines Super Guppy 201s were acquired in

the early 1970s. These proved to be so effective that a further two Boeing Stratocruisers were similarly modified by French company UTA Industrie in 1982-83, thus doubling the Airbus Industrie fleet.

After flight testing the assembled A300s, completed aircraft were flown to Hamburg for interior fitting out, then returned to Toulouse for painting and handover to the customer.

The prototype Airbus A300B1 first flew on 28 October 1972, powered by two General Electric CF6-50A turbofan engines. Only two B1s were built, as the larger B2 was quickly chosen as the standard production model. Longer, and with an increased gross weight, the prototype B2 completed its maiden flight on 28 June 1973, and subsequently entered service with Air France in May of the following year. The production life of the B2 was to be short-lived, however, as it was soon superseded on the various production lines of Europe by the B4, which carried more fuel in order to boost the airliner's range. More powerful CF6-50C engines were used to power this variant, which proved to be very popular with Asian carriers.

The British re-entry into the Airbus consortium coincided with the development of the

Virgin Atlantic Airways' A340-300 fleet now numbers ten aircraft, with G-VHOL and G-VSEA (only the second and third examples of the A340 to be built) having been used by Airbus Industrie between 1992 and 1997 for their own development work on the new jetliner. Once these trials had been completed, both aircraft were totally refurbished and sold to Virgin. Although a year younger than the two development aircraft acquired by the airline from Airbus in 1997, G-VBUS Lady in Red was actually the first A340 delivered to Virgin in 1993. This photograph was taken at a frosty London/Gatwick on 16 December 1993, and it shows the factory-fresh jetliner being towed to its gate at the airport in order to be readied for its next service

A310. Initially dubbed the A300B10, the aircraft utilised the same wide-body layout as the earlier Airbus, but featured a redesigned wing and seating for just over 200 passengers. The initial variant was to have been the -100, but this was dropped and the General Electric CF6-80A-powered -200 became the standard production version instead. The prototype completed its maiden flight on 3 April 1982, and production examples had entered service with Lufthansa and Swissair by the spring of 1983 – the latter carrier's A310s are powered by Pratt & Whitney JT9D-7R4E engines.

The -200 series was followed by the long-range -300, this variant being easily recognisable thanks to its distinctive winglets. First flown on 8 July 1985, the -300 has since been joined within the A310 family by the multi-purpose -200C Combi and dedicated -200F Freighter.

Whilst this smaller member of the Airbus family was being introduced to the market, development of the A300 continued, resulting in the introduction of the series -600. This aircraft was longer than its predecessors and had an increased capacity, but thanks to the greater employment of composite materials within its structure, the jet's overall 'weight gain' was kept

to a minimum. The first -600 was flown on 8 July 1983, with Saudia acting as the launch customer.

Further evolution of the larger A300 saw the introduction of the -600R extended range version, the first of which flew on 9 December 1987. This was followed by the -600C Convertible and -600F Freighter – the latter has been ordered in quantity by freight 'giants' FedEx and (more recently) United Parcel Service.

While production of the wide-bodied A300 and A310 continued, the manufacturer developed a new product in the shape of the narrow-body short/medium range A320. The first prototype took to the skies on 22 February 1987, and has since been joined on the production line by larger and smaller cousins in the shape of the A321 and A319, respectively. Final assembly of the A319 and A321 is undertaken at the Finkenwerder facility at Hamburg, whilst A320s come together alongside other Airbus Industrie products at Toulouse. The author is currently working on a companion volume to this tome focusing on Airbus narrow-bodies (A319, A320 and A321), and this is scheduled for publication in March 2000.

Having produced a family of aircraft that effectively took the fight to Boeing and

McDonnell Douglas designs in the small and medium-sized airliner markets, the one goal remaining for Airbus was to produce a truly long-range intercontinental jetliner – enter the A330 and A340.

Easily the largest designs to emanate from the European consortium, both models had actually been conceived as long ago as the early 1970s, when they had been given the prospective designations A300B9 and B11 respectively – as noted earlier, the A300B10 had gone on to become the A310. Like all other Airbus types, considerable commonality existed between the two new designs to the point where the series -300 of both models have identical fuselage dimensions and use the same wing. Indeed, the fuselage cross-section of the long-range jets is shared with the A300/A310, whilst the fin for both designs is modelled again on the vertical surface used by the A310/A300-600. Finally, the A330/A340 relies on the fly-by-wire flight controls and cockpit avionics of the A320, thus allowing operators to introduce common pilot ratings which significantly reduces training costs.

The programme was formally launched on 5 June 1987 on the back of commitments for 130 aircraft – 89 A340s and 41 A330s. The twin-jet A330 was aimed primarily at high-density regional routes, whilst the longer range four-engined A340 was specifically designed for intercontinental flight. Two variants of each type were planned, namely the series -200 and -300, and as previously mentioned, the latter have identical dimensions despite the numerical difference in engines. As with the remaining wide-bodies in the Airbus range, A330s and

This aerial view of the Toulouse plant shows just a small area of the final fitting out ramp, with single examples each of the A300-605F (FedEx) and A330-320 (Korean Air), and two each of the A320-210/-230 (Air Jamaica and MEA-Middle East Airlines respectively) and A340-310 (Virgin Atlantic and Philippines Airlines) (Airbus Industrie)

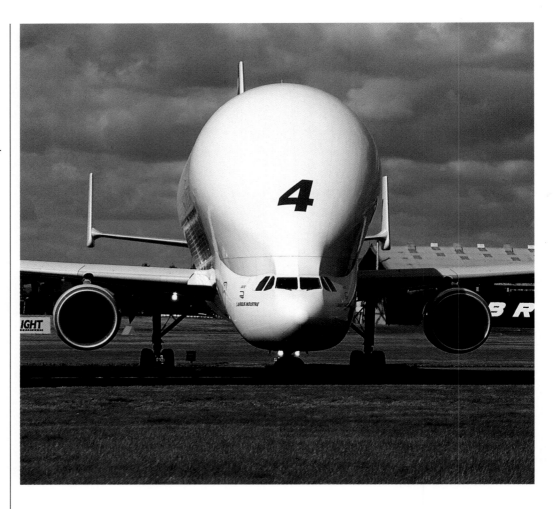

A340s undergo final assembly and flight testing at Toulouse.

Due to customer demand, Airbus chose to develop the A340 first, and the prototype (a series -300) completed its maiden flight on 25 October 1991. The first A340-200 followed on 1 April 1992, and Lufthansa became the premier operator of the A340 in March 1993. The maiden flight of the prototype A330-300 took place on 2 November 1992, with the type entering service with Air Inter just three months later.

The main competitors to the A330/340 family were the McDonnell Douglas MD-11 and the Boeing 777. The MD-11 was initially the market leader, racking up some substantial orders from airlines seeking to replace their veteran DC-10s. However, when it became apparent that the trijet was failing to meet its advertised range,

cancellations started to pour in (see the author's *McDonnell Douglas Jetliners* and *Tri-Jets* volumes in this series for further details). Singapore Airlines was one such customer, cancelling an order for 20 MD-11s and turning to the A340 instead – as with earlier Airbus products, Asia has again proven to be a good market for the company.

With the A340-200/-300 and A330-300 all firmly established and selling well, Airbus finally turned to the development of the smaller A330-200. Formally launched on 24 November 1995, the prototype flew for the first time on 13 August 1997 and entered service with Toronto-based operator Canada 3000 Airlines in May 1998.

Despite the structural commonality between the A330 and A340, one area where they differ greatly is in their respective engines. The A340 is powered exclusively by derivatives of CFM International's CFM56 turbofan, while the A330 has been certified for no fewer than five different engines – the General Electric CF6-80, Pratt & Whitney PW4164 or PW4168, and Rolls-Royce Trent 768 or 772.

Unlike its earlier wide-bodies, Airbus has so far refrained from producing convertible and freighter variants of the A330/A340. The company has, however, developed the A340-500, -600 and -8000, the former designs being given the formal go-ahead at the 1997 Paris Airshow. Utilising more powerful Rolls-Royce Trent engines, the -500 will feature a slight increase in fuselage length over the -300, while the -600 will be significantly longer. Both variants will also be fitted with a larger, redesigned, wing. The first -600 is due to fly early in the year 2001, and enter service with launch customer Virgin Atlantic the following year. The -500 will follow soon afterwards.

As the last of the three new A340 derivatives announced to date, the -8000 will look identical to the series -200 from the outside, but internally will benefit from larger fuel tanks at the expense of capacity, thus giving the new jetliner a greater range.

One of the great selling points of the A330/A340 has been its outstanding fuel economy. The A340 can carry more belly cargo than the 747-400, and although slightly slower in the cruise than the Boeing product, on a non-stop flight from Hong Kong to London, the A340 will burn some 40 per cent less fuel than the 747. A fuel saving of this magnitude has proven to be a significant deciding factor for several customers who compared the merits of Boeing and Airbus aircraft on their respective long-haul routes. In these times of competitive ticket pricing and increased fuel costs, it is also the sort of figure which immediately attracts the eyes of company accountants!

Our examination of Airbus wide-bodies would not be complete without a look at the forthcoming A3XX. Aside from being the largest commercial airliner ever built when it finally enters production sometime next century, it will also form the final 'piece' of the Airbus Industrie 'jigsaw'. At last there will be a competitor to the 747-400 in a market that Boeing has had to itself for far too long.

The innovative four-engined A3XX will be of ovoid shape, featuring a double-deck layout. Several variants are envisaged from the 550-seat A3XX-100, capable of flying from London to Singapore, to the larger 660-seat series -200. Other variants could include an 800 seater, while the manufacturer has not forgotten one of the largest growth areas in the industry – freight. To this end, Airbus has already had discussions with industry 'giants' such as FedEx.

A further 19 international airlines have also been approached by the manufacturer in order to canvas their general requirements for the proposed passenger variants. A leviathan like the A3XX could, and will, cause problems with regards to airport infrastructure, and Airbus has also been in consultation with airports and equipment manufacturers. The aircraft is currently planned for service entry in 2003, with formerly staunch Boeing customer British Airways rumoured to be acting as launch customer.

In September 1998 Airbus announced the sale of its 3000th airliner, and that year's sales should come close to, or even exceed, those of Boeing. A strong Airbus Industrie is vital to both the airlines and the airline industry as a whole, and now that McDonnell Douglas has been subsumed into Boeing, the European consortium is the only civil aerospace manufacturer standing in the way of a Boeing monopoly – and the inevitable price rises that would follow. However, with an ever-increasing market share for its small, medium and large designs, Airbus Industrie looks well placed to 'take the fight' to Boeing come the new millennium.

Airbus A300

Construction of prototype A300B1 F-WUAB began at Toulouse in September 1969, the aircraft subsequently taking to the air on its maiden flight from Airbus Industrie's primary site on 28 October 1972. Powered by two General Electric CF6-50 engines, the aircraft spent its short career performing development and test flights that proved the overall soundness of the design. The second, and final, B1 (F-WUAC) employed CF6-50C engines and flew for the first time on 5 February 1973.

After 18 months of development flying, F-WUAC was refurbished and sold to Belgian charter carrier Trans European Airways, with whom it entered service as OO-TEF on 25 November 1974. This proved to be the only B1

to operate commercially, being configured for 302 passengers. This pioneering aircraft was ultimately retired from service on 1 December 1990, having completed 31,035 hours and 14,946 landings.

Following in the wake of the B1, Airbus commenced series production with the A300B2, which featured an increase in gross weight and a fuselage lengthened by 8 ft 9 in (2.65 m). The first B2 flew on 28 June 1973, and like the second B1, spent the early part of its career on development flying from Toulouse, before eventually being refurbished and sold into commercial service. However, unlike the B1, this aircraft is still flying today with Sogerma and CNES, which are part of the French space agency. Flown on a regular basis, it is an impor-

With the original Airbus logo displayed prominently on its tail, prototype A300B1 F-WUAB is seen during an early test flight from its Toulouse base (Airbus Industrie)

tant 'training tool' for would-be astronauts, who are subjected to weightlessness within the aircraft for periods of up to 25 seconds thanks to a dedicated flight programme that creates conditions of negative g-force – a similar effect is achieved by NASA's veteran KC-135, which performs this task for potential American astronauts. Like the older Boeing jet, the A300B2 has been dubbed the 'Vomit Comet' by those who have flown in it!

Air France became the premier customer for the A300 when it took delivery of its first B2 on 10 May 1974, the airline immediately putting the aircraft into service on its Paris-London/Heathrow route. Just 56 examples of the B2 were subsequently built, including 13 B2K aircraft fitted with Krüger flaps on the leading edge of the wing root (as designed for the B4). Giving the aircraft improved performance for operations from 'hot and high' airports, this variant was acquired by Japan Air System and South African Airways (SAA), the latter receiving its first example on 15 November 1976 – these aircraft are still in service with SAA today. French domestic carrier Air Inter also acquired a single B2K.

The B2 was followed into production by the

A300B4, which shared the dimensions and capacity of the earlier Airbus. The new version did, however, feature increased gross weight and fuel capacity, which significantly enhanced the airliner's range. The first B4 (and ninth A300 built) completed its maiden flight on 26 December 1974, and the first customer delivery was made to Germanair the following year. Although initial sales were principally achieved in Europe, it was in Asia where operators found the type most appealing. Indeed, by the 1980s the B4 was in service with China Airlines, Garuda, Japan Air System, Korean Air, Malaysian Airlines, Philippine Airlines and Thai International.

Its service with China Airlines in particular

RIGHT *French domestic carrier Air Inter used A300s on numerous services, including the high-density routes between Paris-Lyon and Marseilles-Nice. To avoid congestion at Charles de Gaulle airport, the airline was based at Orly, leaving the former to Air France. Air Inter was eventually subsumed by the national carrier, and although it initially operated as Air Inter Europe, it lost its identity once and for all in 1997. The aircraft featured here on approach to Orly in August 1992 is A300B2 F-BVGE, which had initially served with Air France between 1975 and 1982, before being transferred to Air Inter. It remained with the airline for a further 14 years until being retired in 1996 and scrapped*

LEFT As a subsidiary of Air France, Air Charter has for a number of years operated as the charter division of the national carrier, although it has also utilised its aircraft on some scheduled services when required to do so. In latter years the fleet has been very much Airbus orientated, with the A300, A310 and A320 all seeing employment in Air Charter colours. Despite many years of successful service, the company has sustained heavy losses during the mid to late 1990s, and as this volume went to press, Air Charter was expected to be dissolved at the end of 1998. A300B2 F-BVGT was seen at London/Heathrow in full Air Charter livery while operating on behalf of Air France in July 1994

LEFT Air Liberté is an airline in transition. This once proud independent carrier suffered several unprofitable years in the mid 1990s which brought to the brink of collapse, but at the last minute the airline was taken over by British Airways, and is now in the process of being merged with the British carrier's other French acquisition, TAT. Once the two concerns have been combined, the latter name will disappear, and Air Liberté will operate as a BA franchise carrier in BA-style livery. This shot, taken at Orly in June 1995, shows one of two A300-600Rs (this is F-GHEG) operated by Air Liberté whilst still an independent carrier. Today, neither Airbus remains in service with the airline

was most interesting, the Taipei-based company also acquiring a pair of Boeing 767-200s at the same time (in the early 1980s) to operate alongside the European product, and thereby undertaking an unofficial 'fly-off' between the two types, with passenger appeal being a significant factor taken into consideration. At that time I happened to be living in the region and flew numerous sectors on A300s which, from a passenger point of view, I found very appealing – spacious, plenty of legroom and quiet. I think China Airlines made the correct decision when it decided to dispose of its 767s and acquire further A300s. Today, the airline also operates ten -600Rs alongside its A300B4-220s, the final one of these (B-18502) having been delivered to the company as recently as 1997.

The A300 also made an impact in Boeing's 'back yard' when Eastern Airlines, Continental and Pan American acquired the type in varying numbers. As an added sales feature for US customers, Pratt & Whitney's JT9D-59 and, sometime later, PW4000 engines were certified for use on the A300.

In order to further capitalise on the sales success of the basic B4, Airbus introduced two new derivatives – the C4 Convertible and F4 Freighter, with a side-loading cargo door and strengthened floor. Neither variant sold particu-

RIGHT *Lufthansa has always been a strong supporter of Airbus products, with the A330 so far being the only type not to have been ordered by the German flag carrier. The A300B2 and B4 variants originally operated by the airline during the 1970s and 80s have long since gone, although the company still utilises 13 A300-600s, two of which are the long-range variant. Seen here about to depart runway 09R at London/ Heathrow in June 1993 is A300-600 D-AIAP Donauworth, which entered service with Lufthansa in 1987. This aircraft is marked up in the colours of Lufthansa Express, which was a relatively short-lived, low-cost, operation since dispensed with. Painted on the rear fuselage of D-AIAP is the smiling bear logo of the City of Berlin which was created to support the city's (failed) bid to host the 2000 Olympic Games*

LEFT *The only Airbus products operated by Finnair are a pair of A300B4 aircraft, the first of which was acquired second-hand in December 1986. Immediately after their acquisition both aircraft were leased to, and operated by, subsidiary KarAir on charter services. They duly returned to the Finnair fleet on 1 February 1992, and became regular visitors at Mediterranean and Canary Islands airports on charter services. In 1998 both aircraft were sold to new charter operator Air Scandic which, despite the name, is a British airline. Seen whilst still very much a Finnair aircraft, A300B4 OH-LAB was photographed just seconds away from landing at Las Palmas in March 1994*

BELOW LEFT *Monarch Airlines received the first of its four A300-600R aircraft in March 1990, and the type has since been used both on high-density European routes and transatlantic services to Florida. To supplement the Airbus 'twins', a leased DC-10-30 was acquired in March 1996, whilst an MD-11 leased from World Airways operated transatlantic services from Manchester during the 1998 summer season. A pair of A330-200s will join the fleet in 1999, and their arrival may spell the beginning of the end for the quartet of A300s in Monarch service*

RIGHT *Translift Airways was formed in 1991, and it initially operated DC-8s on charter services from its Dublin base. The company's association with Airbus products began in December 1995 following the acquisition of veteran ex-Hapag Lloyd and Air Inter A300B4 EI-CJK, which is seen on the runway at Gatwick a year later. Only the 20th Airbus ever built (sistership EI-TLB was the 12th A300 produced), this aircraft first entered service as long ago as 1975. Note the engine thrust reversers deployed and wing-mounted air brakes. For the past two summers this aircraft (and A300B4-100 EI-TLB) has operated on behalf of Brussels-based charter company Sobelair*

larly well, however, the C4 being bought in small numbers by Japan Air System, Kuwait Airways, South African Airways and Thai International, whilst Korean Air became the sole customer for the Freighter.

The A300 design was significantly revised in 1980 with the development of the series -600, which featured winglets. This version was given the formal go-ahead on 16 December 1980, with Saudia duly becoming the type's launch customer.

The -600 is longer than earlier variants, and has the rear fuselage section designed for the A310. The potential weight increase associated with the greater passenger (267 in mixed layout to 361 in a high-density configuration) and freight capacity on offer with the -600 was offset by the added use of composite materials, which significantly reduced the aircraft's weight to the point where the new Airbus became an attractive alternative to other manufacturers' well-established wide-body designs.

The first -600, powered by JT9D-7R4H engines, flew on 8 July 1983, and the type subsequently entered service with Saudia some nine months later. The CF6-80C2 engine was also certified for use with the aircraft, and this has proven to be the more popular choice of powerplant during the jet's 14 years in production.

Airbus Industrie built the last B4 in May 1984, thus bringing to an end a run of 248 aircraft (including B2s) constructed over a ten-year period. All attention then turned to its replacement, the A300-600.

The first variant to follow on from the 'second generation' A300 was the extended-range -600R. Announced in the mid-1980s, the prototype aircraft completed its maiden flight on 9 December 1987 and entered service with launch customer American Airlines the following spring. Like its predecessors, the -600R has found a market ready and waiting in Asia, and many of the region's Airbus operators were quick to place deposits for the new variant. Their lead was followed across the globe, and by the end of 1998, over 220 -600/-600Rs had entered service.

Despite the disappointing response to the C4/F4 models in the late 1970s, Airbus nevertheless tried again with both concepts come the new -600, but poor sales were realised once more. Indeed, apart from a small order from Kuwait Airways, the sole customer for the -600C4 has been the Amiri Flight of the Abu Dhabi government.

Until very recently, there had been only one customer for the -600R Freighter – namely par-

BELOW LEFT *Translift has not only recently changed its name to TranAer International Airlines, but also shifted the emphasis of its business from charter work to operating mainly on behalf of other carriers. By the end of the 1998 summer season, the airline's fleet comprised 16 Airbus types – nine A320s and seven A300B4s. As an example of its new business strategy, during 1998 four of its A320s were operated on behalf of Britannia Airways in their full livery. The airline also flies services on behalf of Air France, and in 1999 will establish a base of operations in Cologne. TranAer International Airlines has also announced that it is to move some aspects of it operations from Dublin, centralising them instead at London/Gatwick. Caught on camera at the latter location in December 1997 is A300B4 EI-TLL.*

RIGHT *After 17 years of service, Alitalia withdrew its fleet of A300B4s in 1997 and sold a number of the aircraft off for freighter conversion. Boeing 767s, which are supplemented by A321s, have replaced the A300s on high-density routes. Photographed taxying to its gate at London/Heathrow in July 1992 is I-BUSG, which carries the name CANALETTO below the European Union flag aft of the forward passenger door*

cel giant Federal Express. Granted, that order comprised an impressive 36 aircraft, and when they all are finally delivered, it will make the freight carrier the world's largest operator of the A300 – it already boasts the largest A310 fleet, numbering 39 aircraft.

The -600 Freighter received a huge boost in September 1998 when FedEx's great rival United Parcel Service (UPS) placed an order for 30 such aircraft, with an option on a further 30 F4s. These are the first Airbus products to be acquired by UPS, and they will almost certainly be used as replacements for the company's large fleet of veteran DC-8-71s and -73s.

At the other end of the scale, CityBird of Belgium has also placed an order for two -600F4s, making it the first European customer for any of the C4/F4 variants.

As airlines across the globe have started to replace their early A300s with more modern Airbus products, an increasing number of B4s are being converted into freighters to help satisfy the demand in a growing market. This is achieved through the fitment of a freight door in the forward fuselage and the strengthening of the now bare cabin floor – the latter is also covered with rollers to ease the handling of freight. A300B4s have become a popular choice for cargo conversion not only because of their capacity, but also their quiet noise signature, which enables them to operate at night into many noise-sensitive airports.

Major operators such as Channel Express, DHL, Heavylift and TNT already utilise fleets of A300 airliners that have been converted into freighters, whilst a further 50 aircraft on the cusp of retirement from airline service have been earmarked for such conversion – this work is undertaken in several locations, including the British Aerospace facility at Bristol/Filton and DASA's plant at Finkerwerder.

Apart from the Boeing 747-400F, the accolade for the ultimate freighter originally derived from an airliner must go to the A300-600ST Super Transporter, which has been nicknamed the *Beluga* (after the white-coloured cetacean which shares its distinctive shape) and the 'Super Flipper'. Built specifically for Airbus Industrie as a modern replacement for their ageing Super Guppy fleet, the aircraft had to be able to convey outsized cargo between the company's manufacturing and assembly plants scattered across Western Europe.

Based on the A300-600, the *Beluga* has a cavernous fuselage accessed by a large forward-opening door above the cockpit, which has been lowered in order to ease access to the cargo area. For aerodynamic purposes, stabilisers are

BELOW LEFT *Iberia has been operating the A300 on both European and domestic high-density services since 1981, its current fleet of six B4-120s and two B4-200s ranging in age from 17 to 20 years. The airline also operates an elderly mix of DC-10-30s and Boeing 747-100 and -200Bs, although the former are due for replacement by a further batch of A340s, which are on order to join eight already in service. The A320 is also a popular member of the Iberia fleet, some 22 having been in service since 1992. This number is set to increase dramatically in the near future, as the airline has recently placed a further order with Airbus for a follow-on batch of A320s to replace Iberia's still-substantial fleet of Boeing 727-200 Advanced tri-jets – 28 aircraft built between 1972 and 1979. Returning to the A300, this photograph shows the youngest B4-120 presently in service with Iberia coming in to land at London/Heathrow in December 1997. EC-DNR ORDESA was delivered to the Spanish carrier in 1982*

Olympic Airways has just celebrated its 20th anniversary of A300 operations, having taken delivery of the first of eight B4s in February 1979 – six aircraft remain in use today, the two oldest examples having been replaced by a pair of brand new -600Rs in 1992-93. Devoid of the carrier's traditional blue cheatline and tail markings, A300B4-200 SX-BED TELE-MACHUS is seen rolling onto the runway at Athens, bound for London, in May 1996. The sole -200 in the fleet, this aircraft is also the oldest A300 presently flying with Olympic Airways, having been only the 58th Airbus built by the consortium

located at the end of the horizontal tailplanes and a 'fillet' has been added to the leading edge of the vertical tail fin, although the latter still looks undersized. The end result is an aircraft which, when first seen, brings forth comments such as 'how can that thing fly?'

But fly it indeed does, the *Beluga* boasting twice the capacity of the Super Guppy, and of course a considerable speed advantage over its ageing predecessor. The first aircraft flew on 13 September 1994 and entered service in January 1996, and today, four of the five on order are regularly flying with Super Airbus Transport International (SATIC), which is a subsidiary of Airbus.

A mark of the aircraft's success has been the many chartering enquiries received by SATIC for their outsized freighters, although until the optional fifth machine has been delivered, most of these have had to be turned down. Even rival Boeing has resorted to chartering the *Beluga* to transport aircraft parts and sections to Boeing Field when the American manufacturer was in a rush to increase its production rate – the trans-

BELOW *Second-hand A300s have proven popular with Turkish charter airlines, although such carriers tend to spring up one day and be gone the next! Akdeniz Airlines is one such example, having started operations on 1 June 1995 with two former Eastern and Continental Airlines A300B4s. Akdeniz failed to last even until year's end, however, its aircraft being taken over by fellow Turkish operator Onur Air. A300B4 TC-TKB ONUR KAZIM was photographed at London/Gatwick in July 1995 during a rare visit to Britain*

RIGHT *Another Turkish A300 operator that enjoyed only a brief existence was GTI Airlines, which was formed in 1996 with two A300B4s and a single B2 to operate services between Germany and Turkey – the initials 'GTI' stood for German Travel International. The airline has since changed its name to Air Anatolia, and is based at the coastal resort of Antalya. Seen in GTI markings in August 1997 at London/Gatwick whilst operating a sub-charter is former Air Jamaica A300B4 TC-GTB*

BELOW RIGHT
Formed in 1992, Air Alfa soon tapped into the lucrative market for transporting Turkish guest workers to and from Germany – there are over a million such individuals in the latter country. The airline also carries tourists from Western Europe to the increasingly popular Turkish holiday resorts. A pair of leased Airbus A321s (which had briefly operated with British West Indian International Airways) now supplement the fleet of five A300B4s. Seen climbing out of Amsterdam's Schiphol airport in August 1995, A300B4 TC-ALP suffered a groundfire whilst parked on the ramp at Istanbul airport on 17 May 1996 and was subsequently written-off

porter flew parts normally shipped to Seattle from Wichita by rail. Surprisingly, Airbus generated little publicity for their leviathan from this heaven-sent opportunity.

Returning to the standard A300, assembly of the series -600 range continues at Toulouse, although orders have now dropped to a steady trickle as airlines instead look towards the A330/A340 and the Boeing 777 to fulfil their needs – as of 30 September 1998, a total of 518 A300s of all variants had been ordered, 474 of which had been delivered, with 434 currently in service.

Although the A300's days are numbered on the production lines of Europe (at least in airliner form), Airbus Industrie would not be where it is today without the enduring success of the design.

Indeed, it does not seem that long ago that the A300 was the 'new kid on the block', but it has been around so long that an increasing number of older aircraft have been withdrawn from use at the end of their useful lives and simply broken up for scrap both in Europe and the USA.

BELOW *Egyptair's A300s were daily visitors to London/Heathrow airport prior to the airline acquiring more modern A340s and Boeing 777s in 1996-97, and it is these later types which now predominate on the Cairo route. The airline originally bought eight A300B4s in the early 1980s, although the first of these was lost in a crash in September 1987. All but two of this batch have now been disposed of following the introduction of nine A300-620R variants in 1990-91. SU-GAR ZOSER, seen in the carrier's old livery in December 1992, was the first of the -620Rs delivered to Egyptair*

RIGHT *Apart from the recently-introduced Boeing 777s, Emirates has a fleet dominated by Airbus products, and this pattern is set to continue with the recent order for 17 A330-200s and six A340-500s. The Dubai-based airline currently operates a fleet of six -600Rs (the first of which was delivered in May 1989), nine A310-300s and seven 777-200s. Emirates usually serves both London/Heathrow and Gatwick with their 777s, although the Airbus types can sometimes be seen at the latter airport. Taxying for departure at Gatwick in January 1991 is A300-600R A6-EKE*

BELOW RIGHT
Following the loss of much of its fleet, and infra-structure, in the 1991 Gulf War, Kuwait Airways has steadily rebuilt its operation through the purchase/lease of some 23 airliners from the Airbus and Boeing stables – the former include the A300, A310, A320 and A340. The A300 fleet comprises a single A300-600C4 convertible freighter and five -600R long-range aircraft, with 9K-AME AL-RAWDHATAIN (seen here taxying for departure at London/ Heathrow in January 1995) being the last example delivered in 1993

LEFT *Qatar Airways underwent a radical management changeover towards the end of 1996, which resulted in several routes being dropped, a revised fleet plan and even a new livery. Its Boeing 747s, which had filled the Far East-London/Gatwick via Cairo route, were relegated to charter work, and a pair of appreciably smaller A300-600R aircraft leased to operate direct services to London/ Heathrow instead. Why the airline should switch to Heathrow, where it has to compete head-on with British Airways, remains a mystery. The airline will soon be introducing two A330s onto this route to replace the A300-600Rs. A7-ABN is seen taxying to its gate at Heathrow's Terminal 3 after completing a flight from Doha*

Pakistan International Airlines (PIA) acquired four new A300B4-200s in 1979-80, and the acquisition of second-hand examples has since seen the fleet double in size. During the aircrafts' long service with PIA, they have been used primarily to connect Pakistan with regional Asian destinations such as Bangkok, where AP-BEL was seen in March 1995. The youngest B4-200 in the Pakistani fleet, this aircraft had originally been delivered to Singapore Airlines in 1983, before operating briefly with Luxair and South African Airways

Immaculate-looking A300-600C4 A6-PFD is one of two such aircraft used as VIP 'shuttles' with the United Arab Emirates/Abu Dhabi Amiri Flight. Other types employed by the flight include the Falcon 900, BAe146-100 and Boeing 747SP

ABOVE *South African Airways' fleet of seven A300s comprises three different variants, namely a single C4-200 all-cargo aircraft, four B2K-200s built specifically for operations from hot/high airfields, and two B4-200s. One of the latter is ZS-SDE SPRING-BOK, which is seen at its Jan Smuts Airport (Johannesburg) base in March 1996*

LEFT *China Airlines has been an A300 operator since 1982, when it took delivery of its first B4-220 variants. Six of these are still in service with the airline, operating alongside ten newer -620R models. B4-220 B-1810 is seen at Kai Tak in the airline's old livery in August 1986*

BELOW LEFT *There are few A300 operators on the African continent, with the latest being Nigeria's Bellview Airlines. The carrier commenced operations in 1992, and presently owns just a pair of elderly DC-9 aircraft. A single A300-600R was added to the fleet through a lease arrangement in November 1997, the Airbus having seen service with Garuda Indonesia for the previous five years. Resprayed in Bellview's blue and white scheme and registered as 5N-BVU, the aircraft inaugurated a new service to Nairobi, but during the latter part of 1998 it was spotted at several airports operating services on behalf of other African carriers – it is here seen at London/ Heathrow fulfiling a scheduled Ghana Airways service to Accra in September 1998*

China Airlines has the unhappy distinction of having lost two -600Rs during a decade of service, with both aircraft crashing in very similar circumstances – stalling on final approach apparently due to pilot error. One was lost near Nagoya, in Japan, on 26 April 1994 and the other on finals to the airline's base at Taipei on 16 February 1998. The second aircraft lost was 1990-veteran A300-620R B-1814 which, as flight CAL676 from Bali, crashed after its crew initiated a go-around when in the final stages of approach to runway 05L at Taipei's Chiang Kai Shek International, killing all 196 on board and six on the ground. The aircraft concerned is illustrated here in the airline's current livery at Hong Kong's Kai Tak airport three months prior to its tragic demise

RIGHT *Shanghai-based China Eastern Airlines operates ten A300-600Rs both on high-density domestic services and on regional Asian routes. This view of B-2320 (delivered in 1993) on short finals to runway 13 at Kai Tak in November 1994 is dominated by the imposing Lion Rock in the background. In 1995 China Eastern Airlines became the first operator in China to fly the A340*

BELOW RIGHT *Airbus products are steadily increasing in numbers on the Chinese register thanks to the passenger appeal of wide-bodies like the A300. One of the company's newest customers is China Northern Airlines, which has operated five -620Rs alongside a large fleet of MD-82 and MD-90 aircraft since 1993-94. These are flown in a two-class configuration of 24 first and 250 economy seats, being allocated to high-density services between major population centres. A300-620R B-2315 is seen waiting to depart from Beijing in March 1997*

Below *Philippine Airlines was one of the many Asian carriers who selected the A300 in the mid-1970s, the type entering service with the airline just in time for the busy Christmas period of 1979. Over the years second-hand leased examples took the A300 fleet to a maximum strength of ten aircraft, although only nine are presently operated. Other Airbus types like the A320, A330 and A340 have since joined the fleet, but the manufacturer is likely to have to find new customers for many of those aircraft yet to be delivered, for a damaging pilots' strike exacerbated an already perilous financial situation and forced the airline to cease operations on 23 September 1998. Limited services started again several weeks later, but it would appear that the ageing A300s have no future with the beleaguered airline. Adorned in the current livery, A300B4-200 RP-C3003 (delivered in 1980) approaches Kai Tak in November 1994*

RIGHT *China Northwest Airlines is also an operator of Airbus products, having steadily replaced its fleet of uneconomical Russian-built aircraft with Western European jetliners. For example, the airline is currently in the process of receiving A320s in place of its Tu-154M fleet, despite the latter jets having only been delivered between 1986 and 1990. Short-haul services are undertaken by nine BAe146 aircraft, while three A310s and five A300-600Rs service long-haul domestic and regional routes. Here, 1994-build -600R B-2324 leads a China Eastern MD-82 to the holding point at Beijing/Capital airport in March 1997*

Right *GrandAir is another Philippino carrier which is suffering financial woes as a result of the economic crisis in the Far East. Several times during its brief existence it has been forced to suspend operations, with the latest halt grounding its modest fleet in September 1998. The airline has operated a small number of 737-200s and A300B4 aircraft since the mid-1990s, the latter including French-registered F-OHPN leased from Airbus itself. Seen here at Kai Tak in November 1997 servicing the Manila-Hong Kong route, this aircraft previously served with Greek operator Apollo as SX-BAY*

F-OHPN

RIGHT *Thai Airways has been a valued Airbus customer over the years, having operated the A300 continually since 1977. The airline initially received 12 B4-100/-200s, one of which was subsequently converted to C4 Convertible standard. Seven of the B4s remain in use today mainly on domestic routes, while the larger A300-600 serves in greater numbers. Six basic -600s and ten -600R/-620Rs undertake regional routes, with a further five of the latter version still on order with Airbus. Thai's splendid, and innovative, livery looks outstanding in the late afternoon sunshine as A300B4 HS-TGH SRIMUANG taxies to the gate at Kai Tak in August 1986*

LEFT *In contrast to Thai International's colourful Orchid livery seen opposite, A300-600R HS-TAH NAPACHINDA appeared in late 1994 with this modified livery, which featured a grey cheatline – fortunately the idea did not catch on! The last -600R delivered to the airline (in 1989), HS-TAH is seen at Kai Tak in November 1994*

BELOW LEFT *Korean Air is presently the second largest Asian operator of the A300, with 31 airframes currently in service. The airline was an early customer for the Airbus, commencing operations with the B4 in 1975 – just one A300B4-100 remains in the inventory today, HL7219 having been delivered 24 years ago. Korean Air later served as the launch customer for the F4 freighter, two of which are in use. The bulk of the Airbus fleet is made up of the longer -620/-620R variant, with no fewer than 28 currently wearing Korean Air blue. All but five of these are the long range -620R variant, and one such aircraft – HL7580 – is seen about to land at Osaka/Kansai in April 1998*

Japan Air System (JAS) was the first and, until very recently, only operator in the country to order Airbus products. Having flown A300B4-200s since 1980, JAS has the world's largest fleet of A300s in passenger configuration — a fact which goes some way to counter national carrier Japan Air Lines almost embarrassing loyalty to Boeing products. With just a solitary -620R still to be delivered as this book went to press, JAS's Airbus fleet is presently comprised of 19 A300-620Rs, nine B4s and eight A300B2K-200s. With the recent introduction of MD-90s and Boeing 777s, JAS unveiled a new rainbow-inspired livery, the airline having previously adopted the Airbus house colours to coincide with the introduction of the A300. Illustrating this scheme is A300B4-200 JA8292 (delivered in 1980), seen at Osaka's Itami airport in April 1988

RIGHT *Prior to having its name changed simply to Australian Airlines, Trans Australian Airlines received four A300B4-200 passenger aircraft and one freighter in 1982-83. After the take-over by flag carrier Qantas in October 1993, the aircraft were subsumed into their fleet and repainted in the overall white scheme. Seen coming in to land at Sydney in Australian Airlines colours in February 1993, VH-TAD had the distinction of performing Qantas's final A300 flight on 24 October 1998 when it completed a scheduled return service as QF459 between Sydney and Melbourne. A total of 196,816 hours were flown by the five-strong fleet, and the surplus aircraft have reportedly been sold for freighter conversion*

RIGHT *American Airlines (AA) currently operates the world's second-largest fleet of A300s, with some 35 -600Rs (delivered between April 1988 and February 1993) on strength. Almost exclusively operated between North and Central American destinations, AA A300s have recently found themselves in European skies following the airline's capacity shortage on its transatlantic services due to the premature sale of its MD-11s to FedEx. Introduced on some of the shorter transatlantic routes such as Boston-London, the aircrafts' primary employment remains on domestic and Central American routes, with Miami being one of the type's hubs – rotating from runway 27L at Miami in*

January 1997, A300-600R N40064 (delivered in 1988) is seen wearing AA's all-over grey scheme, as opposed to the airline's more common natural metal finish

ABOVE LEFT Formerly known as Federal Express, cargo giant FedEx has so far taken delivery of 28 of the 36 A300F-605R freighter variants is has on order. Operating from its huge Memphis hub, FedEx covers virtually every corner of the globe with its diverse fleet of 630 aircraft, which includes large numbers of A300s, A310s, DC-10s, MD-11s and Boeing 747s. A few A310s operate from a new hub at the former US Navy base at Cubi Point in the Philippines, but the A300s are generally restricted to domestic routes. Only the third ever A300F-605R delivered (in 1994) to FedEx, N654FE is seen about to land at San Diego in September 1996

RIGHT *Dominicana has operated several A300B4s, although all have been on a short-term lease basis. One such aircraft was this former Eastern Airlines and Pan American Airbus, which is seen wearing the serial V2-LDX and still adorned in the Latin American carrier's colour scheme, despite being devoid of Dominicana titling. This photograph was taken at Gatwick in July 1992 whilst the aircraft was operating with European Airlines*

RIGHT *In the early days Airbus experienced difficulty penetrating the South American market which, in the 1970s and early 1980s, was dominated by second-hand US types. However, limited sales were eventually achieved, with Venezuelan flag carrier Viasa being one such customer. Tracing its history back to 1961, Viasa had begun to suffer serious financial problems by the mid-1990s, and despite investment from Iberia, it was forced to cease operations on 23 January 1997. Prior to its collapse, Viasa had undertaken international services with two A300B4s and five DC-10s, the former having been ex-Lufthansa aircraft acquired in August and September 1987. The second of these (YV-161C) is seen on the taxiway under threatening skies at Toronto in June 1994*

LEFT *An increasing number of older A300s have been earmarked for freighter conversion, and it would appear that many of these jets will have a long career ahead of them in this role. An early customer for the converted airliner is Channel Express, who have dubbed it the Eurofreighter. The airline has three B4-200Fs in service, with more likely to follow, whilst fellow British cargo carrier Heavylift also operates a solitary example. Both companies regularly undertake freight work on behalf of some of Europe's major airlines, Channel Express, for example, performing regular flights between Stansted and Tel Aviv for British Airways. G-CEXC is seen soaking up the sun at Luxembourg's Findel airport in August 1997, the light picking out the aircraft's freighter door just aft of the forward passenger door*
(Matthew Martin)

ABOVE RIGHT *General Electric CF6-80C2A8 engines power the amazing A300-600ST Beluga, which has also been dubbed 'The Super Transporter' by Airbus. Note the upward-hinging freight door, which is located above the aircraft's cockpit*

ABOVE FAR RIGHT
The cavernous fuselage of the Beluga can accept a variety of outsize items including fuselage sections and complete wings. The first Beluga flew on 13 September 1994 and entered service in January 1996

BELOW *A300-600ST Beluga/Super Transporter No 4 F-GSTD is seen taxying at Farnborough in September 1998. Note how the cockpit has been 'dropped' to a lower position to allow an upward-hinging cargo door to be fitted, thus facilitating easier loading/unloading*

LEFT *The Beluga is fitted with vertical stabilisers at the end of the horizontal tailplanes, these devices improving the lateral control of the slab-sided aircraft at lower speeds*

Airbus A310

Although at first glance the A310 appears to be little more than a shorter version of the A300, there are significant differences between the two types. Granted, it has the same fuselage cross-section as its older cousin in order to allow it to accommodate the same LD3 cargo containers as carried by the A300, but its British Aerospace-designed and built wing is completely different – the aircraft also employs a smaller horizontal tail.

At its inception, the new Airbus was initially designated the A300B10, but by the time of its launch on 6 July 1978 in the wake of strong support from both Lufthansa and Swissair, it had been redesignated the A310. Seating 280 in high density configuration, or around 218 in a mixed layout, the initial variant was to have been designated the -100, but this was dropped and the first production version became the A310-200.

Prototype A310-200 F-WZLH (the 162nd aircraft built by Airbus) took-off from Toulouse on its maiden flight on 3 April 1982, Pratt & Whitney JT9D-7R4D1 engines as specified for its eventual owner Swissair (as HB-IPE) powering this aircraft. Joint launch customer Lufthansa, however, selected the CF6-80A engine instead, whilst a third engine in the form of the PW4000 would also later become available. Both Swissair and Lufthansa put the type into revenue service in April 1983, and global sales of the A310 were soon achieved in numerous markets, including Asia, Eastern Europe and the USA.

As with the A300, the manufacturer introduced two alternative variants, namely the -200C Convertible and -200F Freighter, although neither version proved successful. Indeed, only one -200C was delivered – to Martinair of Holland – in November 1984, and no orders were ever received for the -200F. Despite the failure of the dedicated cargo variants, second-hand ex-passenger A310s have found a ready market with FedEx, in particular, the American cargo operator having acquired a large number of surplus Delta, KLM and Lufthansa jets in recent years. Converted into freighter configuration by FedEx, they now operate alongside the company's equally large fleet of A300s.

Ironically, Martinair's solitary A310-203C has also been bought by FedEx and converted into a freight-only fit. With 36 aircraft in its inventory, FedEx possesses the world's largest fleet of A310s.

As with the A300 before it, the first revision of the A310 saw the resulting series -300 aircraft boasting an increased maximum take-off weight and additional fuel in the fin to allow it to achieve a greater range. The new variant was given the formal go-ahead in March 1983, and the prototype subsequently completed its first flight on 8 July 1985 – following the completion of the flight test and certification programme, this aircraft was sold in January 1989 to Air Niugini, with whom it still serves.

One final fitment available with the A310-300 was the installation of an additional fuel tank in a section of the cargo hold, Wardair of Canada being the first customer to specify this feature.

As with the series -200, Swissair was the first airline to put the -300 into service, although the carrier has recently replaced all its A310s with A330s.

One of the great selling points of the A310 is its endurance, the -200 having a greater range than any variant of the A300 apart from the -600R, while the range of the A310-300 exceeds even that of the larger twin, resulting in the type being used by some carriers on transatlantic services.

With this attribute in mind, it seems obvious that the A310 would make an ideal in-flight refuelling tanker. Indeed, Airbus has looked at a tanker/transport variant of the A310, but to date has been unsuccessful in its attempts to win orders for such a variant. However, the Royal Air Force will soon have a requirement for a new tanker/transport to replace its ageing VC10/Tristar fleet, so all is not yet lost.

The A310 does, however, 'serve in uniform'

with the air forces of Canada, France, Germany, Belgium and Thailand. Four of these countries operate ex-airline aircraft in the transport role only, with the French machines replacing veteran Douglas DC-8s, the Canadian and German examples taking over from Boeing 707s and the two Belgian Air Force A310s recently acquired from Sabena acting as replacements for ageing Boeing 727s. Finally, the Royal Thai Air Force has a single new-built A310 on strength, which is used as a VIP transport on behalf of the Thai Royal Family.

Orders for the A310 have now virtually dried up, with only one received in 1997 and, as this book went to press, none at all in 1998.

Despite the paucity in orders, the type still 'technically' remains in production, although aircraft are now only built to order. As of 31 October 1998, a total of 261 aircraft have been ordered, of which 255 have been delivered and 251 remain in use. The four 'missing' aircraft have all been lost in tragic accidents.

The first of these to crash was Thai International's A310-304 HS-TID, which struck mountains while descending into Kathmandu on 31 July 1992, killing all 113 passengers. The second loss occurred in a highly-publicised incident on 23 March 1994 when A310-300 F-OGQS of Aeroflot crashed while en-route from Moscow to Hong Kong, killing all 75 passengers and crew on board. Accident investigators believe the captain's son, who had been invited up to see the cockpit and briefly fly the aircraft, triggered the crash by causing errant control inputs that effectively disconnected the autopilot servo from the aileron linkage.

On 31 March 1995 Tarom A310-300 YR-LCC crashed near Bucharest/Otopeni Airport soon after taking off for Brussels, killing all 49 passengers and 11 crew on board. Investigators found that this accident was caused by the starboard engine failing to respond to the automatic throttle system's instructions to reduce power. Instead, it maintained full take-off power while the port engine was apparently cut to idle by the the automatic throttle. This gross imbalance in thrust levels quickly rolled the aircraft onto its back and caused it to dive upside down into the ground at an angle of 80°.

Finally, just as this volume was going to press, Thai International suffered a second A310 crash when HS-TIA was lost attempting to land in bad weather at Surat Thani airport in south-west Thailand on 11 December 1998. Of the 144 passengers and crew aboard the jetliner, 101 were killed in the crash. At this point in time the cause of the accident has not been made public.

LEFT *The A310 entered service with Lufthansa at around the same time as it did with Swissair, the German flag carrier acquiring both the series -200 and -300. All of the former have now been disposed of (including two sold to the Luftwaffe), but eight A310-300s remain in service, including 1989-build D-AIDH Wetzlar, which is illustrated inbound to London/Heathrow in October 1995*

BELOW LEFT *One of Germany's oldest charter carriers, Hapag-Lloyd celebrated its 25th birthday in 1997. The airline's fleet of 28 aircraft is dominated by relatively new Boeing 737-400s and -500s, although the replacement of these with Next Generation series -800s has already started. Seemingly unaffected by this change is Hapag-Lloyd's fleet of eight 'middle-aged' Airbus A310s (built between 1986 and 1991), which carry out the company's high-density and long-range services. The A310 fleet currently stands at four -200s, three -300s and a solitary -320. Amongst the former is D-AHLZ, which was delivered new to the airline in March 1988 and is seen here about to land at Las Palmas in March 1994. The easy way to differentiate between a series -200 and a -300 is to check for the winglets fitted to the latter variant. However, Hapag-Lloyd has retrofitted all its A310-200s with winglets as well, thus effectively blurring the external differences between the two types!*

RIGHT *KLM Royal Dutch Airlines has been a loyal and long-established customer of both Boeing and McDonnell-Douglas, its present fleet comprising ten MD-11s and a mix of 737s, 747s and 767s. Despite the Fokker-VFW workshare within Airbus Industrie from the start of the European joint venture, the only sale made to the airline was for ten A310-200s in 1983, which served for 13 years until being disposed of in 1996. Seen here with the thrust reversers already deployed, PH-AGC Albert Cuyp was photographed on touchdown on runway 06 at Amsterdam/Schiphol Airport in September 1992*

LEFT *Dutch charter airline Martinair took delivery of the first of two A310-200s from Airbus in March 1984, the second of which was the sole Combi variant ever built. These aircraft went on to supplement 747s, 767s and DC-10s on both short- and long-haul services until their disposal in November 1995 to FedEx, and subsequent conversion into freighters. Named after Prins Bernhard of the Dutch Royal Family, PH-MCA rotates from runway 24 at Schiphol in September 1994*

BELOW LEFT *Sabena acquired a pair of A310-200s in early 1984 and added a single -300 three years later. The trio of aircraft were used primarily to supplement DC-10s on the carrier's extensive African services until their retirement in 1997 – the -200s were sold to the Belgian Air Force. A330s and A340s now service the carrier's long-haul routes, whilst the Boeing 737 fleet is due for replacement by Airbus's narrow-body A319/A320/A321 family. Photographed at Brussels in August 1996 looking rather the worse for wear in a faded rendition of Sabena's old livery is A310-200 OO-SCA*

RIGHT *Air France took delivery of its first A310 in 1984, and the fleet has remained generally unchanged ever since. Six -200s and four -300s are currently employed mostly on long-haul 'thin' routes such as Paris-Toronto, where the type has replaced the bigger Boeing 767. As a result of this operational change Air France A310s are rare visitors to European destinations such as London/Heathrow, where they were once seen on a regular basis. A310-200 F-GEME was photographed at Heathrow in June 1993 prior to being assigned to the long-haul routes*

LEFT Austrian Airlines received the first of its four A310-300s at the end of 1988, and immediately put the aircraft to work on its long-haul services to Chicago, New York and Tokyo – hence the names of three of the A310s. OE-LAD Chicago is seen at Geneva in March 1996 during a brief stopover on a transatlantic flight from Vienna. Austrian Airlines now also operates A330s and A340s on its expanding route network

BELOW LEFT The A310 was the first Airbus product acquired by TAP Air Portugal, the airline having since added further products from this manufacturer – namely the A319, A320 and A340. Like its peninsular neighbour Iberia, the TAP Air Portugal will soon have an almost exclusively Airbus fleet. The five A310-300s purchased by the Portuguese carrier were delivered between 1988-90, with this particular aircraft (CS-TEX, seen approaching Heathrow in October 1992) being the last to arrive

RIGHT *The most recent Spanish charter airline to appear on the scene goes by the unlikely name of Air Plus Comet. Formed in 1996, the company operates a pair of A310-300s, although one aircraft seems to spend much of its time undertaking sub-charters for other carriers. During the 1998 summer season the aircraft operated services for a number of British carriers who often found themselves short of capacity, or with an aircraft unserviceable at an overseas destination. British Airways even employed an Air Plus Comet jet on a few occasions on transatlantic services. With a large sticker on the rear fuselage encouraging tourists to visit the Andalucia region, A310-300 EC-GOT was photographed during a regular visit to Gatwick in May 1998*

BELOW RIGHT
Founded in 1986, Oasis International Airlines operated MD-83s and A310s on European charter services to Spanish holiday resorts for a decade, before ceasing operations in December 1996. The company's jets initially wore a variety of different tail colours prior to standardising on the dark blue seen here on A310-300 EC-FNI at Gatwick in August 1993

BELOW *Turk Hava Yollari Turkish Airlines operates 14 A310s (seven -200s and seven -300s), which were delivered between 1985 and 1991. Initially used on both European and long-haul services, the aircraft have been almost totally replaced on the latter routes by five A340s, leaving the A310s to concentrate on domestic and European flights. A310-200 KIZILIRMAK is seen about to land at Heathrow in August 1997*

RIGHT *The politically-divided island of Cyprus is populated in the north by those of Turkish extraction, and with the support of the Turkish government, the islanders have formed their own airline – Kibris Turk Hava Yollari (KTHY). Greatly assisted by THY, the company commenced operations in 1974, and today it operates both Boeing 727s and A310s from its Ercan base. The A310 fleet consists of two aircraft – a series -200 and a -300, the former being on lease from Air France. Christened ERENKOY and registered TC-JYK, the -200 is seen at Heathrow in May 1998*

BELOW RIGHT *The remainder of the island of Cyprus has an allegiance to Greece, and Cyprus Airways' current fleet is comprised solely of Airbus products. The first of four A310-200s was acquired in 1984, with eight A320s following from 1989 onwards, although three of the latter operate in the colours of charter subsidiary Eurocypria Airlines. Captured on film poised for touchdown at Gatwick is A310 5B-DAX ENGOMI. Don't be fooled by the series -300 winglets, for this aircraft is actually a series -200 – it is the only A310 within the fleet to have been fitted with them*

BELOW LEFT *To the west of Cyprus is the smaller Mediterranean island of Malta, which also possesses its own airline. Air Malta commenced operations with two leased Boeing 720 aircraft in 1974, and today the airline's inventory is comprised predominately of Boeing737s, supplemented by a pair of Airbus A320s. In the mid 1990s a leased A310 was also seasonally acquired to increase capacity in the busy summer months. Former Lufthansa A310-200 D-AICM was used during the summer of 1994, and it is seen at Heathrow right at the end of its lease in December of that year. Soon after completing its spell with Air Malta, the A310 was sold to FedEx and converted into a freighter*

RIGHT *In recent years the A310 has proven to be a popular choice for emerging airlines in the former Soviet Union, with their selection perhaps being influenced by Aeroflot's decision to acquire the aircraft in 1992. The Russian national carrier initially acquired five leased A310-300s, and has since increased its complement of the type to ten, with a further two to follow. Aeroflot suffered a high-profile loss of an A310 in March 1994 when F-OGQS crashed in Siberia whilst en-route to Hong Kong following mishandling by the pilot's son, who was being shown the controls by the crew. Seen preparing to depart Hong Kong's Kai Tak airport is F-OGQU SKRIABIN, which was a sister-ship of the lost A310*

RIGHT *Diamond Sakha Airlines began operations with a pair of leased ex-Pan American A310-200s from its base at Yakutsk, in the Russian Far East, in October 1994 . Despite the vast distance between Yakutsk and London, these aircraft have been regular visitors to Heathrow airport ever since, operating flights for Aeroflot – a small Aeroflot sticker is just visible on the nose of winglet-equipped A310-200 F-OGYN, seen approaching Heathrow in August 1997. The airline has since changed its name simply to Sakha Airlines*

RIGHT *Armenian Airlines began operations in 1993 with a fleet of Tupolev Tu-134s, Tu-154s and Ilyushin Il-86s. A service from Yerevan to London/Gatwick was started in the summer of 1998, initially with Il-86s, but this was soon replaced by leased A310-200 F-OGYW ARARAT. The aircraft was photographed during its inaugural trip to the London airport on 2 August 1998*

LEFT *Tarom acquired the first of three A310-300s in December 1992, and they are presently the only long-haul type in the airline's inventory. These aircraft are also employed on some European services, and it was actually on a flight from Bucharest to Brussels that Tarom's YR-LCC was lost soon after take-off on 31 March 1995, killing all on board. Sister-ship YR-LCB Moldova is seen here about to land at Heathrow in December 1997*

RIGHT *Uzbekistan Airways has a large fleet of jet airliners of Soviet extraction, namely Tu-154s, Il-62s and Il-86s, plus Il-76 freighters. In recent years three western types have also been added, although in very small numbers. In 1997 three Avro RJ85s were acquired, one of which is a VIP aircraft, and a pair of Boeing 767s have also recently joined two A310-300s which were acquired in 1993. In 1998 a third A310 was acquired by Uzbekistan Airways from Airbus, this aircraft being the only brand new example delivered last year. Here, A310-300 F-OGQY displays the airline's colourful livery as it taxies clear of the runway at Heathrow at the end of a flight from Tashkent in July 1994*

BELOW FAR LEFT
Although only formed in 1985, Emirates Air has built up an enviable reputation for its in-flight service, amassing a number of awards. The airline initially commenced operations with a leased Boeing 737 and a former government 727, simultaneously placing orders for new A300s and A310s with Airbus. The company operates six and nine aircraft of these types respectively, while no less that 17 A330s are also on order. The last of nine Boeing 777s has recently been delivered, and they operate services to both London's Gatwick and Heathrow airports, although the Airbus types are also occasionally used on these routes. One such occasion occurred on 27 January 1998 when A310-300 A6-EKI flew into Gatwick on a return service from Dubai

BELOW LEFT
Middle East Airlines is one of the last scheduled operators of the Boeing 707, and the type will soon be withdrawn completely, leaving the airline with an all Airbus fleet. In 1997 it acquired on lease two A320s and two A321s to supplement its five-strong fleet of A310s. Three of the latter aircraft are ex-Singapore Airlines series -200s, whilst the remaining pair are series -300s leased from GECAS. One of the latter is F-OHLI, seen at Heathrow in October 1996 painted in the airline's old, but well known, livery

RIGHT *To coincide with the relaunch of services from the now rebuilt Beirut airport, which was devastated during many years of fighting, Middle East Airlines adopted a new, but rather staid, livery. It is believed Airbus Industrie assisted the airline in choosing its 'new look', and this is likely to be true as the manufacturer has a penchant for favouring boring, predominately all-white, schemes! Indeed, with the red fuselage stripe, tail flashes and titling all gone, only the three-colour 'MEA' lettering and revised cedar tree logo disrupt the otherwise white fuselage and tail. This scheme is displayed on A310-300 F-OHLI, photographed on approach to Heathrow in August 1997*

BELOW LEF

in 1963 as Alia - Royal
Jordanian Airlines, the
company adopted its
current livery in 1986, and
at the same time dropped
the Alia prefix from the
title. The aircraft types in
the airline's inventory have
remained unchanged for
many years, with two A320-
210s acquired in 1990 and
a third example in 1995
being the last aircraft
introduced. Two veteran
Boeing 707-320C freighters
are still employed, as are
the five L-1011-500
TriStars bought in 1981-82.
The four A310-300s and
two -200s (the latter on
lease from Air Algerie)
operate most of the
European routes. Royal
Jordanian's livery is certainly
unusual, but nevertheless
very attractive, with the
gold crown, in particular,
standing out against the
charcoal background. The
scheme is shown to good
effect on A310-300
F-ODVH PRINCE
HAMZEH at Heathrow
in March 1993

Amongst the aircraft hastily acquired in the wake of the 1991 Gulf War were five ex-Wardair A310-300s, which served for two years before being sold to Polaris Leasing when the airline took delivery of four new examples from Airbus. Having previously served with Wardair as C-GJWD, A310-300 A6-KUD is seen undergoing night maintenance at Gatwick in October 1992. This aircraft can be seen in its current guise as F-OHLI of Middle East Airlines on pages 68-69

RIGHT *Yemenia - Yemen Airways currently operates two leased A310-300s which joined the fleet in March 1997. Prior to their arrival, the airline had briefly flown an A310-200 for some six months in 1995. That aircraft, (F-OHPQ) is illustrated in the airline's attractive livery at Gatwick in June 1995, waiting to depart for Sana'a via Rome. This service had previously been operated by Boeing 727s*

BELOW LEFT *Only a handful of African operators have used the A310 over the years, with one of the first to do so being Kenya Airways, who acquired the first of three series -300s in 1986. These aircraft are still in use today as the airline's sole long-range equipment. Christened HARAMBEE STAR, A310-300 5Y-BEN leads an SAS MD-80 onto the ramp at Copenhagen's Kastrup airport in August 1995*

BELOW RIGHT

Formed some years ago, Air Afrique is a rather unique airline in that its represents a consortium of Central and West African countries, rather than a single nation. Despite having successfully traded through the difficult years of the early 1990s, the company was beset by serious financial maladies in 1998. Indeed, these have become so serious that a number of the carrier's aircraft have been either repossessed or returned to the lessor, including all four A310-300s. TU-TAC was seen at Paris/Charles de Gaulle in August 1992

RIGHT *Biman Bangla-desh Airlines is one of the latest operators of newly-built A310s, two of which were acquired in 1996. Bought to supplement the DC-10 fleet on long-haul international services, the first A310-300 delivered was S2-ADE, which was allocated the name* City of Hazrat Khan Jahan Ali *(Airbus Industrie)*

FAR RIGHT *Pakistan International Airlines operates the Boeing 747 alongside Airbus A300s and A310s, although it also uses F-27s and Boeing 737s on domestic routes. The A310 fleet of six -300s have been operating with the carrier mainly on long-haul and regional services since 1991. Seen approaching Athens in May 1996, A310-300 AP-BEC displays the airline's livery, which has remained generally unchanged for years*

RIGHT *Considering the size and population of the country it serves, Air India's fleet of just 28 aircraft of three different types appears to be somewhat on the modest side. Numerically, the Boeing 747 (13 examples) is dominant, supported by three Airbus A300s and eight A310-300s. The latter have been in use since 1986, principally servicing international routes which cannot support a 747. After a brief flirtation with a new colour scheme, the airline returned to its traditional scheme, with palace-type artwork painted around the windows. Seen inbound to Kai Tak in April 1987 is A310-300 VT-EJK* Gomati

The mountain Kingdom of Nepal has experienced a surge in tourism over the past decade, particularly from westerners who wish to trek across the country's scenic terrain. Two Boeing 757s were purchased in 1987 as replacements for a pair of elderly Boeing 727s, and the Boeing twins are used on long-haul services to the Far East and Europe. A single German-registered A310-300 (D-APON) was also leased in December 1993 and operated for two-and-a-half years – it is seen here at Gatwick in June 1994 during one of the twice-weekly services it flew into the London airport

RIGHT *Thai Airways was a domestic carrier which later added a few regional routes to its network, acquiring two A310s to supplement its Boeing 737s and Shorts SD330/360 fleet. However, in 1988 the airline's identity disappeared following its acquisition by the rapidly expanding Thai International, which then became Thai Airways International. Photographed in January 1988 in Thai Airways' attractive livery during pushback at Bangkok is A310-200 HS-TIC*

ABOVE FAR RIGHT

The two former Thai Airways A310s are still in service with Thai Airways International, and are amongst the few series -200 aircraft fitted with winglets. The airline allocates names to every aircraft in its large fleet, with the Thai city of Phitsanulok providing the title for A310-200 HS-TIA, which was lost on 11 December 1998 in a crash which killed 101 passengers

RIGHT *Singapore Airlines received the first of some 23 A310s in 1984, and the aircraft is presently the smallest of the four types in its 87-strong fleet. The A310s are employed on regional services which do not require the higher capacity of the A340, Boeing 777 or 747. Five of the six series -200 aircraft have been disposed of, although all 17 -300s are still in service, including 9V-STE seen at Bangkok in March 1995*

RIGHT *Rarely photographed is anonymous-looking A310-300 V8-HM1, which belongs to the Sultan of Brunei. This aircraft is one of 11 in the Sultan's private fleet, which includes A340s and a Boeing 747, and has been in service since 1987. It was photographed landing at Gatwick in November 1992*

BELOW LEFT *CAAC (Civil Aviation Administration of China) was for many years not just the regulatory body for flying in this huge communist country, but also the major airline in China. In the late 1980s the flying division was broken up and regional carriers formed, with aircraft operated by CAAC being divided up between a number of these new carriers. Amongst those aircraft 'shared out' were five A310s, including -300 B-2304, seen here in the old CAAC livery at Osaka's Itami airport in April 1990*

BELOW RIGHT *Xian-based China Northwest Airlines operates both the A300 and the A310, with three of the latter in service. Two of these aircraft were formerly operated by CAAC, including 1984-build A310-220 B-2302, photographed at Beijing in March 1997*

RIGHT *Formed in 1973, Air Niugini today uses a pair of A310-300 aircraft on services to nearby Australia and further afield. The colourful Bird of Paradise is prominent on the tail of the airline's aircraft, which is in stark contrast to the rather boring white fuselage interrupted only by the titling. P2-ANG was photographed taxying for departure from Kai Tak on a flight to Port Moresby in November 1994*

BELOW RIGHT *Like their counterparts in Spain, charter airlines in Canada have come and gone with great rapidity, with the latest to enter the history books being Air Club International. Formed in 1993, the airline used A310s and Boeing 747s on long-haul charters primarily to Europe in the summer and the Caribbean and southern USA in the winter. Despite several successful years, the Montreal-based carrier finally ceased operations in December 1997. This photograph shows A310-300 C-GCIV about to land at Brussels in August 1996*

BELOW LEFT *Going against the trend, Royal Aviation is a Canadian charter operator which has steadily expanded since its inception in 1991 with Boeing 727s and L-1011 TriStars. The airline acquired the first of four Boeing 757s in 1998, with 737s also joining the inventory following the take-over of Canair. Three A310-300s were acquired on lease in 1997, with a fourth joining the fleet in 1998 to supplement the TriStars on long-haul services. C-GRYV, seen here at Gatwick in September 1997, has previously served with China Eastern, Air Afrique and Oasis*

Wardair was once a famous name in Canadian aviation circles, but sadly disappeared into history following its acquisition by Canadian Airlines International in 1989. Wardair had commenced operations as long ago as 1952, and by the late 1960s had become one of Canada's most successful transatlantic charter operators. During the 1970s and 80s it flew modern wide-bodied types like the Boeing 747, DC-10 and A310, eventually establishing scheduled services including a route linking Toronto with London/Gatwick, utilising the Airbus. Climbing into the crystal clear skies above Toronto in May 1989 is A310-300 C-GDWD

BELOW RIGHT *Delta Airlines is one of America's 'mega-carriers', exclusively operating US-built equipment. Along with fellow 'giant' American Airlines, the company signed an agreement with Boeing to buy only their jetliners at a favourable price. Had a European airline made such an agreement with Airbus Industrie, 'the powers that be' in the USA (i.e. Boeing) would have immediately cried 'foul'! Prior to this deal being struck, Delta did in fact operate the A310 for a number of years, firstly in the shape of 'inherited' Pan American series -200s, followed by new-build series -300s ordered directly from the manufacturer. The airline utilised the latter variant primarily on the 'thin' European routes. They did, however, very occasionally visitor Gatwick when substituting for TriStars. N841AB was photographed on just such an occasion at the London airport in November 1994*

LEFT *Pan American World Airways is a name which will never be forgotten in aviation circles, and this once proud company deserves many accolades for its contribution to civil aviation, and long-haul travel in particular. The airline was at the forefront of US aviation in the early days of the jetliner, introducing into service aircraft like Boeing's 707 and 747. Prior to its sad demise in the early 1990s, the airline had operated both the A300 and A310, with no fewer that 21 of the latter type having been taken on charge (both series -200s and -300s). The A310-300 was used on transatlantic services to some European destinations such as Geneva, from where N815PA Clipper Mayflower is seen departing in April 1991*

BELOW LEFT *Formerly known as Federal Express, US express parcel delivery company FedEx is now the world's largest A310 operator, with 36 of the type in its massive fleet. All are second-hand series -200s acquired mostly from European carriers and converted to freighter standard – FedEx also has seven ex-Pan American/ Delta aircraft. This particular jet (N405FE), seen on approach to Orange County airport in Southern California, is a former Lufthansa machine*

In 1995-96 Air Jamaica took delivery of six leased ex-Delta Airlines A310-300s, using the aircraft to service international routes including London/Heathrow, where colourful N837AB Spirit of Jamaica was photographed on final approach to runway 27L in July 1998

RIGHT *As in Africa, there are very few airlines in South America which operate the A310. One of those which does is LAB-Lloyd Aero Boliviano, who have two series -300s on lease from ILFC. The airline is now an associate of VASP Brazilian airlines, and the Boeing 727 is the mainstay of the carrier's fleet, with nine presently in service. The two A310s are used to service US destinations, including Miami, where CP-2307 was photographed on its rollout on runway 30 in January 1997*

BELOW RIGHT *Only a handful of second-hand A310s currently 'serve in uniform' as general or VIP transports with the world's air forces, the largest operators being the Luftwaffe and Canadian Armed Forces with five aircraft apiece. Designated the CC-150 Polaris in Canadian service, and all originally part of the Wardair fleet., they are presently operated by No 437 'Husky' Sqn at Canadian Forces Base Trenton, in Ontario. These aircraft are regularly used on transportation tasks on behalf of the United Nations, and when undertaking such work, they often carry the UN flag on the fin below the Canadian equivalent. Exhibiting just such a marking is CC-150 15003, seen resting in the evening sunshine at London, Ontario, in June 1994*

LEFT *The cockpit of the Airbus A310-300 mixes traditional dials, gauges and control columns with more modern glass cockpit-like screen displays* (Airbus Industrie)

Airbus A330

I n June 1987 Airbus Industrie proudly announced the joint launch of twin- and four-engined airliners which would tackle rival Boeing and McDonnell Douglas designs in the lucrative long-haul market sector.

Despite the dual unveiling, development of the A330 twin-jet would follow that of the A340, even though the only external difference between the A330-300 and the A340-300 is the number of engines employed. By using just two engines, the range of the A330-300 has been reduced to about two-thirds of that achievable with the A340, although passenger capacity remains unchanged at a maximum figure of 440 in single-class fit, or around 335 in a two-class configuration.

Powered by General Electric CF6-80E1A2 engines, prototype A330-300 F-WWKA lifted off from Toulouse on 2 November 1992. It was joined one month and one day later by the second example, and their development flying included certification work for the Pratt & Whitney PW4164/PW4168 and Rolls-Royce Trent 768/772 engines, which was duly awarded on 21 October 1993.

In January 1994 French domestic carrier Air Inter performed the A330-300's first revenue earning service when it introduced the type on

This photograph of the final assembly hall at Toulouse in March 1997 shows the central fuselage section of the first A330-200 about to be mated with the front and rear sections (Airbus Industrie)

its Paris/Orly-Marseilles route in the 412-seat configuration. Air Inter eventually took delivery of three aircraft, although due to financial problems and the impending take-over by Air France, these virtually new jetliners had left the fleet by the end of 1997. The next customer to receive the A330 was Aer Lingus, who had never previously operated Airbus products.

As with other Airbus wide-bodied types, Asia proved to be a good hunting ground for the manufacturer's sales teams, as Cathay Pacific, Dragonair, Malaysia Airlines and Thai International all became early customers, followed a few years later by Garuda, Korean Air and Philippine Airlines. European sales have been thin on the ground, however, especially after Air France cancelled its order for 15 aircraft. Germany's LTU became the first charter carrier to acquire the type, and they use it on both long- and short-haul services.

As with the A340, penetration into the US market has so far proven difficult, with a Trans World Airlines order for ten machines having been on hold for some time. The company's fortunes in this market have recently been boosted, however, by an order from domestic carrier US Airways for seven aircraft, with options on as many as 23 additional airframes. Deliveries are due to start in December 1999. Meanwhile, the prize for the first North American operator of the type went to Canadian charter airline Skyservice, who acquired a solitary A330-300 in May 1997 for use on services to destinations in mainland Europe.

The latest addition to the Airbus Industrie wide-body portfolio is the A330-200. Launched on 24 November 1995, the -200 has a fuselage length some 5.3 m shorter than its 'big cousin', although it utilises the same wing. Seating capacity ranges from around 253 in mixed configuration to no fewer than 340 in high density fit.

The aircraft also has an additional centre-section fuel tank which, depending on configuration, offers an increase in range over the -300 by between ten and twenty per cent. The combination of this capacity and range makes the A330-200 an ideal alternative to the Boeing 767 (including the forthcoming 767-400 model), and these attributes have made the

The sleek lines and super efficient wing of the A330-200 are shown to good effect in this view of the prototype performing a steep banking turn during its display routine at Farnborough 98. The demonstration flights carried out during the airshow week in September 1998 dramatically proved the outstanding handling qualities of the big airliner, with perhaps the highlight of its seven-minute routine being its slow high-angle of attack flyby

Airbus product a firm favourite with long-haul charter operators.

The prototype A330-200 flew on 13 August 1997 and, unusually, the launch customer for the new variant was a leasing company – global giant International Leasing Finance Corporation (ILFC). Charter operator Canada 3000 Airlines signed-up for the first two aircraft from ILFC, and they entered service with the carrier in early May 1998.

The airline uses them predominately on its European routes, the aircraft having the capability to fly from Vancouver to Athens non-stop. The airline has found passenger response to its wide-body overwhelming, vindicating its decision to acquire an aircraft with a quiet, spacious, cabin that can operate non-stop long-haul services, yet charge charter prices for tickets. A third aircraft will join Canada 3000 in 1999, and fellow Canadian operator Air Transat has also recently placed an order for two examples.

The A330-200 has proven popular with European charter carriers too, with Airtours, Corsair, Leisure International and Monarch all selecting the type.

Turning to non-charter operators, an order has been taken from Emirates, who have signed up for 17 examples, and the type has recently entered service with both Austrian Airlines and Swissair. If this trend continues, the -200 is likely to outsell the -300, and Airbus officials have now publicly admitted that perhaps the -200 should have been launched in advance of the larger variant.

Total A330 orders as of 30 September 1998 stood at 244, with 78 of these yet to be delivered. Not included in these figures is A330-300 F-WWKH, which crashed near Toulouse with the loss of all seven crew members on 30 June 1994 whilst on an air test prior to delivery to Thai International. The resulting inquiry cited aircrew error.

Canada 3000 became the premier operator of the A330-200 when it received its first aircraft (C-GGWB) on 29 April 1998 – the second example on order (C-GGWA) followed a month later. Photographed just nine days after delivery, A330-200 C-GGWA is captured on film as the tyres impact the tarmac of runway 26R at Vancouver, British Columbia. Canada 3000 will add a third A330 on lease from ILFC in 1999. The airline also utilises six A320s and nine Boeing 757s, with the latter supplementing the Airbus wide-bodies on transatlantic services. These A330s are now regular Gatwick visitors, and during the 1998 summer season both jets were regularly seen on the ramp at the same time

RIGHT *The honour of being the first carrier to operate the A330-300 went to French domestic carrier Air Inter, which received the first of its three aircraft on 30 December 1993 and placed them in service on the high density Paris/Orly-Marseilles route just a few days later. Both the A330s and the Air Inter identity have since been disposed of following the airline's acquisition by Air France, who themselves cancelled their order for 15 of the type. A330-300 F-GMDB is seen taxying for departure from Orly in June 1995, this aircraft having been acquired by Sabena in July 1997 following Air Inter's dissolution*

BELOW LEFT *After Air Inter, Ireland's Aer Lingus became the second operator of the A330, the airline ordering the A330-300s to replace its ageing Boeing 747-100s on its transatlantic routes. Due to the aircrafts' frugal fuel consumption, their introduction very quickly turned around routes which had been operating at a loss for several years, and the airline has since increased its fleet to five, with a sixth jet on order. The acquisition of the sixth example will allow the carrier to inaugurate a Dublin/Shannon-Los Angeles service in June 1999. Photographed about to land on runway 31R at New York's John F Kennedy International is A330-300 EI-SHN St Flannan. Aer Lingus has allocated personalised registrations to its A330 fleet that denote the airports the type serves, SHN, for example, being the ICAO three-letter code for Shannon*

RIGHT *The initials LTU stand for Lufttransport-Unternehmen, this Dusseldorf-based charter carrier operating a fleet of Airbus A330-320s, Boeing 757/767 and MD-11 aircraft, although the tri-jets are to be imminently disposed of. The airline took delivery of its first A330-320 in December 1994, and currently flies six of the Airbus twin-jets. It has also signed a lease agreement with ILFC for a seventh A330 which, at the time of writing, is serving with Malaysia Airlines. LTU primarily uses its A330s on European services, including flights to the Canary Islands. Illustrated at the carrier's Dusseldorf base in August 1998 is D-AERH*

BELOW RIGHT *Cathay Pacific will soon receive its 13th A330, making it the world's largest operator of the type. The first example was delivered in February 1995, and the aircraft has effectively replaced the Lockheed L-1011 TriStars that served the regional routes for almost two decades. Cathay Pacific operates its A330s in a 44-business and 270-economy seat configuration. With Hong Kong's transfer back to the People's Republic of China, all of the territory's aircraft have been re-registered with the communist B-prefix. Seen at Nagoya in April 1998 taxying for departure on its return flight to Hong Kong is A330-300 B-HLA, which was formerly VR-HLA*

BELOW LEFT

With its undercarriage
mostly obscured, this shot
of taxying Dragonair
A330-300 B-HYA will
probably not meet with
the approval of the purists.
The aircraft was
photographed taxying
across the bridge from the
remote parking ramp to
the parallel taxyway leading
to the runway at Kai Tak in
November 1997. In the
background a Cathay
Pacific Boeing 747-400 can
be seen on approach, yet to
make its final turn to align
with runway 13. Dragonair
now operates five A330s,
with a sixth yet to be
delivered

RIGHT *A number of Asian carriers are suffering financially due to the dire economic climate in the Far East, with Garuda Indonesia being one of the worst affected. With the virtual collapse of the country's economy and the eventual abdication of President Suharto in 1998, civil aviation in Indonesia has been dealt an almost mortal blow. The massive devaluation of the Indonesian Rupiah against the US dollar has had severe repercussions for Garuda, with new-build Boeing 737s being flown from Boeing Field into desert storage and the entire MD-11 fleet returned to the lessor when the airline could no longer afford the lease payments. Intercontinental services have been slashed, although the London/Gatwick route is still being operated by Boeing 747-400s instead of the MD-11s. Amongst the last types received by Garuda prior to the onset of the economic crisis where six A330-300s, although a further three remain undelivered. PK-GPC was seen at Osaka/Kansai International in April 1998*

LEFT *Korean Air is another of Asia's flag carrier's in deep trouble, although with this airline the problems are not just of a financial nature – Korean Air has a deplorable safety record as well. On top of the tragic loss of a Boeing 747-300 on Guam in 1997, there have been a further three incidents in South Korea in 1998 that have fortunately not resulted in any loss of life. Turning to its use of the Airbus, the airline was an early customer for the A300, and it now also operates two variants of the A330 – one of two series -200s and four out of eleven series -300s have so far been delivered. Photographed rotating from runway 13 at Kai Tak in November 1997 is A330-300 HL7551. Although only the forward pair of wheels on the centre-bogie are clear of the ground, note the flex in the wings as they take the strain of the aircraft's weight*

LEFT *Malaysia Airlines A330-300s are powered by Pratt & Whitney PW4168 engines and operate in a three-class configuration of 12 first, 56 business and 213 economy seats (F12C56Y213). The airline currently operates 12 aircraft, the first of which was delivered in February 1995. Two of these are leased from ILFC, however, and their return to the lessor is imminent. One of those aircraft is 9M-MKY, which is seen here at Beijing/Capital airport in March 1997*

RIGHT *The Asian carrier most badly affected by the economic crisis is undoubtedly Philippine Airlines. After many weeks of industrial action by employees, including pilots (many of whom were ultimately sacked), the country's national airline ceased operations in September 1998. Attempts are ongoing to resurrect the company, and limited international services were resumed on 15 October. As with Garuda, Philippine Airlines had received all eight A330-300s on order prior to its fiscal 'meltdown' — F-OHZS, seen at Osaka/Kansai in April 1998, was the penultimate delivery*

RIGHT *Apart from the recent US Airways order, sales of the A330 in North America have proved disappointing. Continental cancelled an order for 15 aircraft, and both Northwest and Trans World Airlines have placed their orders for 16 and 10 respectively 'on hold'. There are currently just two A330 operators in this vast continent, and both are Canadian charter carriers. Skyservice was formed in 1986 and operates a handful of A320s within North America. On 7 May 1997 it acquired a single A330-300 which had served with LTU for two years. Wearing the appropriate registration C-FBUS, this aircraft is used on transatlantic services to Western Europe, and is seen here on final approach to Toronto in June 1997*

LEFT *In February 1995, Thai Airways International became the first of the Asian carriers to take delivery of the A330-300. To date, ten of the twelve aircraft on order have been delivered, and the operator uses them to supplement A300-600s on regional services. This dramatic shot of HS-TEF SONG DAO sees the aircraft executing a 470° turn onto final approach for runway 13 at Hong Kong's Kai Tak airport, and was taken from the famous 'checkerboard' using a 400 mm lens in May 1998*

Airbus A340

The A340 has the distinction of being the largest aircraft built to date by Airbus Industrie. It was developed alongside the A330, and as mentioned in the introduction to this book, both types share the same fuselage cross-section as the A300/A310. The A330 was destined primarily for high density regional routes, while the A340 would undertake the longer range intercontinental sectors.

Family commonality is a feature of all Airbus products, and the A340 features the same cockpit as the A330. This enables airlines like Cathay Pacific (which operates both types) to save considerable amounts of money on crew training due to the jets sharing common ratings. Both types are also the first wide-bodies to employ the same fly-by-wire flight controls as fitted to the A320 family.

There are currently two models of the A340 available, namely the series -200 and -300, and both are powered by four CFM56-5C2 engines. Although the series -200 is slightly shorter in length than the -300, all remaining dimensions are identical for the two jets. The -200 possesses the longer range, and typically seats 262 passengers in a three-class configuration, although up to a maximum of 420 can be accommodated in a single-class fit. The figures for the series -300 are 295 and up to 440 passengers.

The maiden flight for prototype A340-300 F-WWAI was completed on 25 October 1991, whilst the first -200 (F-WWBA, which was the fourth A340 built) took to the skies on 1 April 1992. The first four aircraft constructed were all kept busy on development and test flying to meet the December 1992 certification date, and

Lufthansa became the first airline to take delivery of the A340 in January 1993, with the type duly entering service two months later. The German carrier is now the largest operator of the big Airbus, with six A340-200s and 11 series -300s presently in use. Another three -300s are due for delivery soon, along with 11 of the larger -600s. Named after the Hanseatic city of Lübeck, A340-200 D-AIBF is seen taxying at Dusseldorf in August 1998

with the completion of the bulk of the development flying for the -300 by 1996, the second and third A340s were totally refurbished and passed on to Virgin Atlantic in 1997.

Perhaps the highlight of the flight trials for the A340-200 was a 16-hour 22-minute non-stop flight from Toulouse to Perth, in Western Australia, at close to maximum all up weight – a quite incredible achievement.

On 15 March 1993 Lufthansa became the first airline to put the A340 into service, with Air France following soon afterwards. The German carrier is currently the largest A340 operator, with a mixed fleet of 17 -200s and -300s in service at the end of 1998. Although sales of the A340 have not been outstanding, a steady series of orders have been secured, with the Asian market once again proving vital for Airbus.

In addition to a significant order from Cathay Pacific, Singapore Airlines opted for the A340 when it realised the MD-11s it had originally ordered would not meet their advertised range specifications. Although sales in the Far East have been good, once again Airbus has found it hard to break into the Boeing-dominated US market

with the A340. Things initially looked promising for the new airliner when Northwest Airlines looked set to take no less than 24 examples, but this order was later cancelled. Indeed, the only A340 operator in the Americas is Air Canada with nine -310s – these have joined over 65 A319s and A320s in service with Canada's largest airline, thus making the operator one of Airbus's best customers.

The A340 has already proved popular as a VIP aircraft for the governments of several oil-rich nations. Egypt, Qatar and Saudi Arabia all operate single examples, with the latter-mentioned country usually assigning its aircraft to its Washington Embassy. Not to be outdone, the world's richest man, the Sultan of Brunei, owns no less than three A340s, two of which operate in Royal Brunei Airlines livery (they are not, however, part of the fleet) presumably for anonymity.

Turning to the future, for several years now Airbus has been looking at developing additional larger and longer-range variants of the A340, but has been constrained by the lack of suitable engines. However, thanks to the recent certifica-

tion of Rolls-Royce's Trent 553 and 556, the manufacturer has been able to at last forge ahead with its series -500 and -600 variants. Announced in June 1997 at the Paris Airshow, the -500 features a fuselage stretch of 4.1 m in comparison with the -300, giving an increased capacity of 313 passengers in a three-class layout or 440 in high-density configuration. The series -600 stretch is much more pronounced at 11.6 m, with a capacity ranging from 380 to 485 passengers.

Aside from lengthening the aircraft's fuselage, Airbus has also had British Aerospace completely redesign the wing to incorporate a span increase of 3.3 m and area increase of 20 per cent. These changes have in turn permitted a 38 per cent increase in fuel capacity. To cope with the greater weight of the jet, the central undercarriage bogie will be changed from a two to a four-wheel unit, which will retract forwards into the fuselage rather backwards. This change of direction will allow the -600 to carry additional cargo in the central lower fuselage area, while the -500 uses the space to house an extra fuel tank.

The combination of the new central tank and additional fuel cells in the wings will allow the -500 to carry an incredible 50 per cent more fuel than the -300. This effectively means that the aircraft will be able to fly non-stop transpacific services, thus becoming the 'champion' long-range airliner. With a fuselage length of 75.3 m, the A340-600 will also become the longest airliner in the world – a title currently held by the Boeing 777-300. When combined, all these characteristics make the new Airbus an ideal replacement for earlier versions of the Boeing 747.

Finally, both the -500 and -600 will have a slightly taller fin, while an increase in wing sweep to 31.50° should see an increase in speed to Mach 0.83, compared with the current figure of 0.82 for the A330/A340. Greater use of carbon-

Following close on the heels of Lufthansa, Air France was the next to put the A340 to work on its route network. In addition to its own series -200/-300 aircraft, the French carrier leased five jets originally destined for Sabena, who were not then in a position to take delivery. These aircraft have now been returned to the Belgian airline, with the exception of the one lost in a groundfire at Paris. Photographed in October 1994 as it taxies onto the ramp at Rio de Janeiro, A340-200 F-GNIE spent three years in service with Air France before it joined the Sabena fleet in April 1997 as OO-SCZ

fibre and composite materials will help keep the overall weight increase down.

Assembly of the first A340-600 will begin at Toulouse early next year, with an initial flight date planned for early 2001. Delivery to launch customer Virgin Atlantic should take place about 12 months later, and the series -500 will follow close behind the -600. At the time of writing eight airlines have placed 53 orders and 65 options for the new models.

As of 30 September 1998, 246 A340s had been ordered, 144 of which have been delivered. Just one A340 has so far been written-off – series -200 F-GNIA of Air France was lost on 20 January 1994 when it was destroyed by fire whilst undergoing maintenance on the ramp at Paris/Charles de Gaulle Airport. Embarrassingly for the French carrier, this aircraft was actually on lease from Sabena at the time!

LEFT With all five Sabena A340s going straight from Toulouse to Air France, enthusiasts had to wait until June 1996 to see the type in the house colours of the Belgian flag carrier. Having failed to replace the lost Air France -200, the airline today operates a modest fleet comprising the surviving pair of -200s and a similar number of -300s. They are used primarily on services across the Atlantic and to Africa. Seen poised for touchdown on runway 01 at Brussels in August 1996 is A340-200 OO-SCX

RIGHT *A worm's eye view of a Virgin A340 about to land at RAF Waddington in May 1995*

BELOW *Turk Hava Yollari - Turkish Airlines is the sole A340 operator in the eastern extremities of Europe. Although Ankara is the national capital, A340 operations are centred on the metropolis of Istanbul, from where the aircraft route westwards to London and New York, and eastwards to locations like Bangkok. Currently operating five aircraft, the airline has a further two A340s on order. A340-300 TC-JDK ISPARTA is seen inbound to London/Heathrow in July 1994*

OPPOSITE *TAP - Air Portugal received the first of its four A340-300s on 22 December 1994, and the type was soon replacing A310s and L-1011 TriStars on intercontinental services. The aircraft was also used to inaugurate a joint service with Sabena from Lisbon via Brussels to the newly-built airport at Macau, which is not far from Hong Kong. The type is also used on services to Africa, including Johannesburg, where CS-TOA is seen taxying to its gate in March 1996*

RIGHT *TAP's neighbouring national carrier Iberia is also an A340 operator. Although the airline had been an early customer for both the A300 and the A320, Airbus Industrie had to wait several years before the Spanish national carrier finally confirmed it had selected the A340 to replace its DC-10s. All eight aircraft ordered had been delivered by 1998, with an additional six on order to supplement the airline's elderly Boeing 747-200s on long-haul services. No doubt Airbus will be doing its best to convince Iberia that the A340-600 is the ideal replacement for the Boeings in the long term. Illustrated at Madrid's Barajas airport in September 1997 is A340-300 EC-GGS* CONCHA ESPINA

BELOW LEFT *Prior to receiving its three A340-200s, Egyptair had leased two Gulf Air series -300s, although these have now been returned to the Bahrain-based carrier. Egyptair also has two A340-600s on order, and these will replace the Boeing 747-300s presently in use. With the introduction of the Airbus long-haul jetliners, the airline revamped its livery by adopting a blue and white scheme, although it retains the logo of Horus, the ancient falcon-headed god. Displaying this livery on approach to Heathrow in May 1998 is A340-200 SU-GBN CLEO EXPRESS*

RIGHT *A look at the Kuwait Airways' fleet list reveals that some ten different types feature within an inventory of just 30 aircraft – this can hardly be conducive to cost effective operations! For long-haul routes, four types are operated, namely the A300-600R, A340-300, Boeing 777 and Boeing 747-200. The airline also maintains a single Boeing 747-400 exclusively for the government, although it is painted in full Kuwait Airways livery. The four A340s were delivered between March and July 1995, and are operated in a three-class F18C24Y238 configuration. Named AL-SABAHIYA, 9K-ANB is seen taxying clear of the runway at Heathrow in September 1998*

RIGHT *A few thousand miles to the north-east of Kuwait lies Sri Lanka, formerly known as Ceylon. In September 1994 Air Lanka became the latest member of the Airbus club, and during the next six months took delivery of all three of its A340-300s, which allowed it to replace its L-1011 TriStars. Based in Colombo, Air Lanka operates eastwards to Hong Kong and as far west as London. A340-300 4R-ADC is seen approaching Heathrow in October 1998*

LEFT *When Qatar's Amiri Flight acquired brand new A340-200 A7-HHK in May 1993, it became the first operator of the VIP variant in the Middle East. The Amiri Flight, which has a fleet of five aircraft including a Boeing 747SP, will be joined in the near future by an A310 and an A320*

OVERLEAF *Cathay Pacific chose both the A340 and A330 to jointly replace its sizeable fleet of L-1011 TriStars, and by so doing became the first Asian carrier to put the type into service. This distinction should have actually gone to Philippine Airlines, but when the time came for them to take delivery of its first four machines in mid-1995, the operator was reluctant to do so due to financial problems. Keen to get hold of A340s well ahead of the expected delivery date for its own aircraft, Cathay Pacific duly took the first four Philippine Airlines' -200s on two-year leases, although these aircraft have now been returned and the Hong Kong-based airline exclusively operates a fleet of 11 series -300s. The second of the leased -200s was VR-HMS, which is seen here taxying at Kai Tak on a lovely sunny morning in September 1995*

VESSELS WITH MAST/DERRICK/CRANE HEIGHTS OF 20M OR MORE
ARE PROHIBITED BEYOND THIS POINT VESSELS MAY NOT APPROACH
CLOSER THAN 120M TO THE AIRPORT RUNWAY PROMONTORY
OFFENDERS WILL BE PROSECUTED

RIGHT *Having deferred the delivery of its A340s, the management at Philippines Airlines decided early in 1996 that it should retire some of its ageing, and fuel-thirsty, Boeing 747s and replace them on European routes with new Airbus aircraft. However, they could not do so when they wanted as the carrier's four A340-200s were on a two-year lease to Cathay Pacific, and the delivery of its four series -300s was nearly a year away! Fortunately for the Asian carrier Gulf Air had several aircraft surplus to requirements, and three were acquired on short-term lease in the summer of 1996. They were quickly put into use on several routes, including the Manila-London/Gatwick service, where Gulf Air A340-300 A40-LC (in full Philippine Airlines livery) is seen about to land on its first trip to the airport on 24 September 1996*

BELOW LEFT *China Eastern Airlines A340-300 B-2380 leads a pair of Boeing 737s down the taxyway at Beijing's Capital airport in March 1997. Airbus has been slow to make serious inroads into the Chinese market, which has for so long been dominated by Boeing and McDonnell Douglas products. Shanghai-based China Eastern Airlines ordered five A340-300s, three of which were delivered between May and July of 1996, with the remaining pair arriving the following year. The airline operates these aircraft in a two-class business/economy configuration of 24 and 251 seats respectively*

RIGHT *Air China's long-haul fleet comprises over 30 aircraft, most of which are Boeing products – two variants of the 767, three versions of the 747 and the 777 just being introduced. Bucking the Boeing long-haul monopoly are just three A340-300s, which were delivered in quick succession in October-November 1997. The first to arrive was B-2385, which is seen here about to land at Osaka/Kansai airport in April 1998. Behind the descending aircraft is the bridge that links the new offshore airport to the mainland*

BELOW RIGHT

Singapore Airlines is the largest Asian A340 operator, having received almost all of its order for 17 A340-300 aircraft. In time these will be joined by five of the ultra long-range series -500s. Singapore Airlines have given type names to some of the aircraft it has operated over the years, such as 'BigTop' and 'MegaTop' for the Boeing 747-300 and -400 respectively. Following this tradition, their A340s have all been named CELESTAR. The type is used primarily on long-range 'thin' routes such as Singapore-Paris, which cannot support a Boeing 747. Here, one of the airline's A340-300s is illustrated during a pre-delivery test flight (Airbus Industrie)

BELOW LEFT *After many years of operating jets solely manufactured in the USA, Air Canada has in recent years become one of Airbus's best customers. Almost 70 A319 and A320 twin-jets are now in service, and the airline took delivery of its first A340s in June of 1995 – a pair of series -300s on lease from ILFC. One of the carrier's A340-300s is seen here during turn-round on gate 54 at Vancouver in June 1998. The operator added additional A340s directly from Airbus Industrie, receiving its first aircraft from Toulouse on 19 November 1996. Air Canada currently has nine A340-300s in its inventory, with a further seven to follow. The airline has also committed itself to both the series -500 and -600, ordering two and three examples respectively*

Appendices

**Airbus Industrie A300-600R
Cutaway Drawing Key**

1 Radome
2 Weather radar scanner
3 Scanner mounting and tracking mechanism
4 VOR localiser aerial
5 Front pressure bulkhead
6 Windscreen panels
7 Windscreen wipers
8 Instrument panel shroud
9 Control column
10 Rudder pedals
11 Cockpit floor level
12 ILS aerial
13 Pitot heads
14 Access ladder to lower deck
15 Captain's seat
16 Centre control pedestal
17 Direct vision. opening sidewindow panel
18 First Officer's seat
19 Overhead systems switch panel
20 Maintenance side panel
21 Observer's seat
22 Folding fourth seat
23 Cockpit bulkhead
24 Air conditioning ducting
25 Crew wardrobe/locker
26 Nose undercarriage wheel bay
27 Hydraulic retraction jack
28 Taxying lamp
29 Twin nosewheels, forward retracting
30 Hydraulic steering jacks
31 Nosewheel leg doors
32 Nose undercarriage pivot fixing
33 Forward toilet compartment
34 Wash hand basin
35 Galley
36 Starboard entry/service door
37 Door-mounted escape chute
38 Cabin attendant's folding seat
39 Curtained cabin divider
40 Forward main entry door
41 Door latch
42 Door surround structure
43 Underfloor avionics equipment racks
44 Runway turn-off light
45 Fuselage lower lobe frame and stringer construction
46 Floor beam construction
47 Cabin window panels
48 Forward freight hold door
49 Cabin wall trimming panel
50 VHF communications aerial
51 Overhead stowage bins
52 Curtained cabin divider
53 First class passenger seating, 26 seats

54 Underfloor air system ducting
55 Door-mounted escape chute
56 Main cabin entry door
57 Overhead stowage bins
58 Central galley unit
59 Starboard General Electric CF6-80C2 engine nacelle
60 Pratt & Whitney JT9D-7A4H1 or PW4156 alternative engine installation
61 Common nacelle pylon beam
62 Pylon attachment links
63 Pylon tail fairing
64 Starboard wing engine pylon
65 Tourist class passenger cabin seating, 241 seats (267 seats total in mixed-class layout)
66 Air system distribution ducting
67 Conditioned air delivery ducting
68 LD3 baggage container, 12 in forward hold
69 Water tank
70 Slat drive shaft motor and gearbox
71 Wing spar centre-section carry-through
72 Ventral air conditioning packs (two)
73 Wing centre box fuel tank
74 Three-spar wing centre-section construction
75 Centre-section floor beams
76 Front spar attachment main frame
77 Fuselage centre-section construction

78 Starboard wing inboard main fuel tank, standard fuel capacity 13,628 Imp gal (62,000 l)
79 Outer wing skin panel joint strap
80 Fuel system piping
81 Pressure refuelling connections
82 Refuelling valves
83 Fuel feed tank and pumps
84 Fuel tank dividing ribs
85 Leading-edge slat drive shaft
86 Three-segment leading-edge slats, open
87 Wing fence
88 Slat screw jacks
89 Outer wing panel integral fuel tank

90 Fuel vent tank
91 Starboard navigation light (green)
92 Wing-tip fairing (green)
93 Starboard wing-tip fence
94 Tail navigation and strobe lights (white)
95 Static dischargers
96 Fixed portion of trailing edge
97 One-piece single-slotted Fowler-type flap, down position
98 Flap guide rails
99 Fuel jettison pipe

100 Outboard roll-control spoilers/lift dumpers (two)
101 Inboard airbrakes/lift dumpers (three)
102 Spoiler/airbrake hydraulic jacks
103 Flap screw jacks
104 Flap drive shaft
105 Starboard all-speed aileron
105 Aileron triplex hydraulic actuators
107 Wing root spoilers/lift dumpers (two)
108 Inboard flap segment
109 Cabin air system recirculation fan
110 Pressure floor above wheel bay
111 Rear spar attachment main frame
112 Starboard main undercarriage, retracted position
113 Undercarriage door jack
114 Equipment bay walkway
115 Undercarriage bay pressure bulkhead
116 Flap drive motor and gearbox
117 Hydraulic reservoir triplex system
118 Eight-abreast tourist class passenger seating
119 Starboard Type 1 emergency exit door

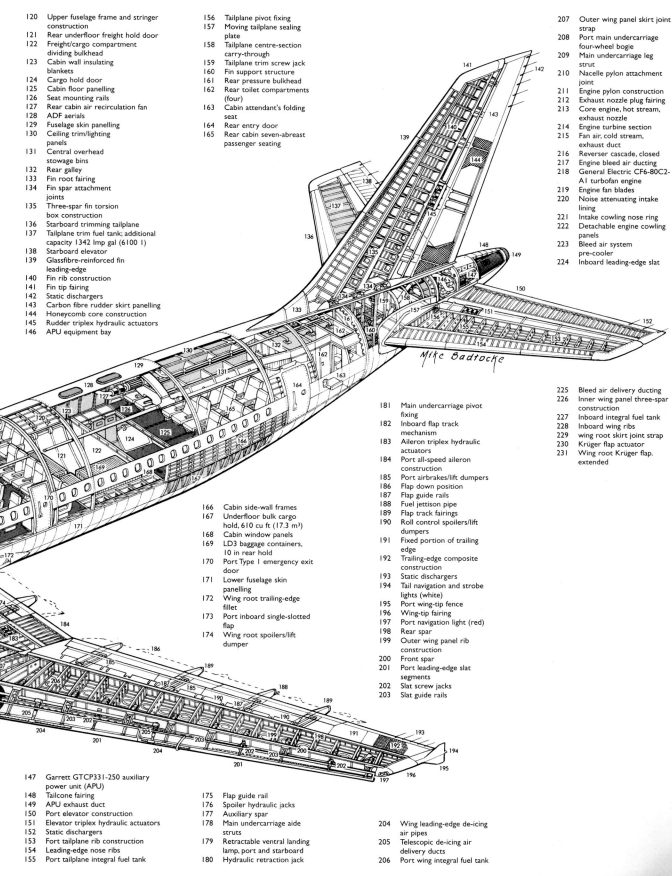

120 Upper fuselage frame and stringer construction
121 Rear underfloor freight hold door
122 Freight/cargo compartment dividing bulkhead
123 Cabin wall insulating blankets
124 Cargo hold door
125 Cabin floor panelling
126 Seat mounting rails
127 Rear cabin air recirculation fan
128 ADF aerials
129 Fuselage skin panelling
130 Ceiling trim/lighting panels
131 Central overhead stowage bins
132 Rear galley
133 Fin root fairing
134 Fin spar attachment joints
135 Three-spar fin torsion box construction
136 Starboard trimming tailplane
137 Tailplane trim fuel tank; additional capacity 1342 Imp gal (6100 l)
138 Starboard elevator
139 Glassfibre-reinforced fin leading-edge
140 Fin rib construction
141 Fin tip fairing
142 Static dischargers
143 Carbon fibre rudder skirt panelling
144 Honeycomb core construction
145 Rudder triplex hydraulic actuators
146 APU equipment bay

147 Garrett GTCP331-250 auxiliary power unit (APU)
148 Tailcone fairing
149 APU exhaust duct
150 Port elevator construction
151 Elevator triplex hydraulic actuators
152 Static dischargers
153 Fort tailplane rib construction
154 Leading-edge nose ribs
155 Port tailplane integral fuel tank

156 Tailplane pivot fixing
157 Moving tailplane sealing plate
158 Tailplane centre-section carry-through
159 Tailplane trim screw jack
160 Fin support structure
161 Rear pressure bulkhead
162 Rear toilet compartments (four)
163 Cabin attendant's folding seat
164 Rear entry door
165 Rear cabin seven-abreast passenger seating

166 Cabin side-wall frames
167 Underfloor bulk cargo hold, 610 cu ft (17.3 m³)
168 Cabin window panels
169 LD3 baggage containers, 10 in rear hold
170 Port Type 1 emergency exit door
171 Lower fuselage skin panelling
172 Wing root trailing-edge fillet
173 Port inboard single-slotted flap
174 Wing root spoilers/lift dumper

175 Flap guide rail
176 Spoiler hydraulic jacks
177 Auxiliary spar
178 Main undercarriage aide struts
179 Retractable ventral landing lamp, port and starboard
180 Hydraulic retraction jack

181 Main undercarriage pivot fixing
182 Inboard flap track mechanism
183 Aileron triplex hydraulic actuators
184 Port all-speed aileron construction
185 Port airbrakes/lift dumpers
186 Flap down position
187 Flap guide rails
188 Fuel jettison pipe
189 Flap track fairings
190 Roll control spoilers/lift dumpers
191 Fixed portion of trailing edge
192 Trailing-edge composite construction
193 Static dischargers
194 Tail navigation and strobe lights (white)
195 Port wing-tip fence
196 Wing-tip fairing
197 Port navigation light (red)
198 Rear spar
199 Outer wing panel rib construction
200 Front spar
201 Port leading-edge slat segments
202 Slat screw jacks
203 Slat guide rails

204 Wing leading-edge de-icing air pipes
205 Telescopic de-icing air delivery ducts
206 Port wing integral fuel tank

207 Outer wing panel skirt joint strap
208 Port main undercarriage four-wheel bogie
209 Main undercarriage leg strut
210 Nacelle pylon attachment joint
211 Engine pylon construction
212 Exhaust nozzle plug fairing
213 Core engine, hot stream, exhaust nozzle
214 Engine turbine section
215 Fan air, cold stream, exhaust duct
216 Reverser cascade, closed
217 Engine bleed air ducting
218 General Electric CF6-80C2-A1 turbofan engine
219 Engine fan blades
220 Noise attenuating intake lining
221 Intake cowling nose ring
222 Detachable engine cowling panels
223 Bleed air system pre-cooler
224 Inboard leading-edge slat

225 Bleed air delivery ducting
226 Inner wing panel three-spar construction
227 Inboard integral fuel tank
228 Inboard wing ribs
229 wing root skirt joint strap
230 Krüger flap actuator
231 Wing root Krüger flap. extended

Mike Badtocke

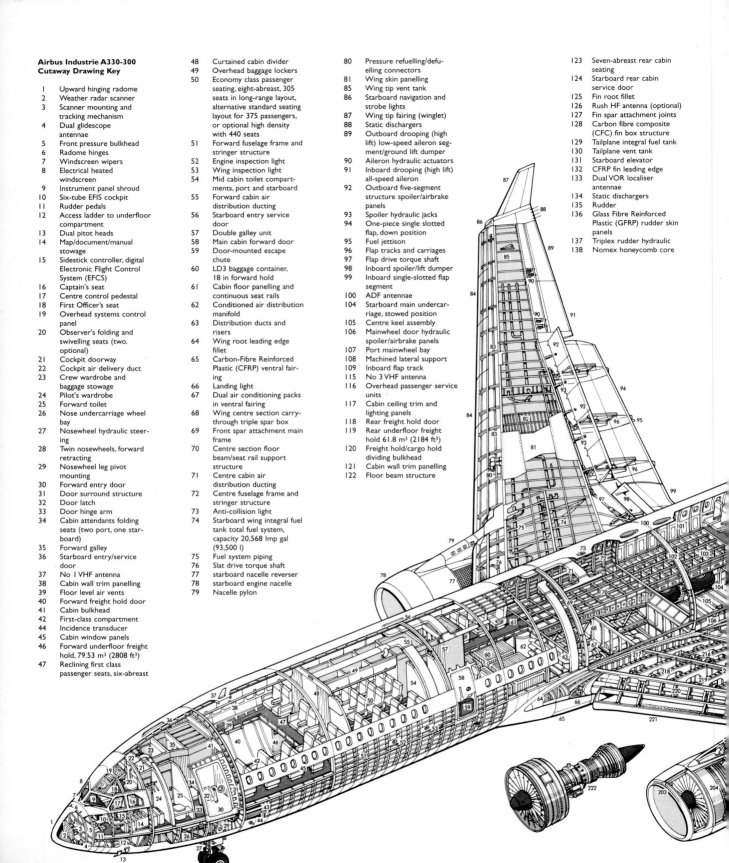

Airbus Industrie A330-300 Cutaway Drawing Key

1. Upward hinging radome
2. Weather radar scanner
3. Scanner mounting and tracking mechanism
4. Dual glidescope antennae
5. Front pressure bulkhead
6. Radome hinges
7. Windscreen wipers
8. Electrical heated windscreen
9. Instrument panel shroud
10. Six-tube EFIS cockpit
11. Rudder pedals
12. Access ladder to underfloor compartment
13. Dual pitot heads
14. Map/document/manual stowage
15. Sidestick controller, digital Electronic Flight Control System (EFCS)
16. Captain's seat
17. Centre control pedestal
18. First Officer's seat
19. Overhead systems control panel
20. Observer's folding and swivelling seats (two. optional)
21. Cockpit doorway
22. Cockpit air delivery duct
23. Crew wardrobe and baggage stowage
24. Pilot's wardrobe
25. Forward toilet
26. Nose undercarriage wheel bay
27. Nosewheel hydraulic steering
28. Twin nosewheels, forward retracting
29. Nosewheel leg pivot mounting
30. Forward entry door
31. Door surround structure
32. Door latch
33. Door hinge arm
34. Cabin attendants folding seats (two port, one starboard)
35. Forward galley
36. Starboard entry/service door
37. No 1 VHF antenna
38. Cabin wall trim panelling
39. Floor level air vents
40. Forward freight hold door
41. Cabin bulkhead
42. First-class compartment
44. Incidence transducer
45. Cabin window panels
46. Forward underfloor freight hold, 79.53 m³ (2808 ft³)
47. Reclining first class passenger seats, six-abreast

48. Curtained cabin divider
49. Overhead baggage lockers
50. Economy class passenger seating, eight-abreast, 305 seats in long-range layout, alternative standard seating layout for 375 passengers, or optional high density with 440 seats
51. Forward fuselage frame and stringer structure
52. Engine inspection light
53. Wing inspection light
54. Mid cabin toilet compartments, port and starboard
55. Forward cabin air distribution ducting
56. Starboard entry service door
57. Double galley unit
58. Main cabin forward door
59. Door-mounted escape chute
60. LD3 baggage container, 18 in forward hold
61. Cabin floor panelling and continuous seat rails
62. Conditioned air distribution manifold
63. Distribution ducts and risers
64. Wing root leading edge fillet
65. Carbon-Fibre Reinforced Plastic (CFRP) ventral fairing
66. Landing light
67. Dual air conditioning packs in ventral fairing
68. Wing centre section carry-through triple spar box
69. Front spar attachment main frame
70. Centre section floor beam/seat rail support structure
71. Centre cabin air distribution ducting
72. Centre fuselage frame and stringer structure
73. Anti-collision light
74. Starboard wing integral fuel tank total fuel system, capacity 20,568 Imp gal (93,500 l)
75. Fuel system piping
76. Slat drive torque shaft
77. starboard nacelle reverser
78. starboard engine nacelle
79. Nacelle pylon

80. Pressure refuelling/defuelling connectors
81. Wing skin panelling
85. Wing tip vent tank
86. Starboard navigation and strobe lights
87. Wing tip fairing (winglet)
88. Static dischargers
89. Outboard drooping (high lift) low-speed aileron segment/ground lift dumper
90. Aileron hydraulic actuators
91. Inboard drooping (high lift) all-speed aileron
92. Outboard five-segment structure spoiler/airbrake panels
93. Spoiler hydraulic jacks
94. One-piece single slotted flap, down position
95. Fuel jettison
96. Flap tracks and carriages
97. Flap drive torque shaft
98. Inboard spoiler/lift dumper
99. Inboard single-slotted flap segment
100. ADF antennae
104. Starboard main undercarriage, stowed position
105. Centre keel assembly
106. Mainwheel door hydraulic spoiler/airbrake panels
107. Port mainwheel bay
108. Machined lateral support
109. Inboard flap track
115. No 3 VHF antenna
116. Overhead passenger service units
117. Cabin ceiling trim and lighting panels
118. Rear freight hold door
119. Rear underfloor freight hold 61.8 m³ (2184 ft³)
120. Freight hold/cargo hold dividing bulkhead
121. Cabin wall trim panelling
122. Floor beam structure

123. Seven-abreast rear cabin seating
124. Starboard rear cabin service door
125. Fin root fillet
126. Rush HF antenna (optional)
127. Fin spar attachment joints
128. Carbon fibre composite (CFC) fin box structure
129. Tailplane integral fuel tank
130. Tailplane vent tank
131. Starboard elevator
132. CFRP fin leading edge
133. Dual VOR localiser antennae
134. Static dischargers
135. Rudder
136. Glass Fibre Reinforced Plastic (GFRP) rudder skin panels
137. Triplex rudder hydraulic
138. Nomex honeycomb core

139 APU air delivery duct
140 APU bay firewall
141 Garrett/ZF/BKT/Turbomeca
142 APU exhaust
143 Port elevator
144 Elevator Nomex honeycomb
145 Elevator GFRP skin panels
146 Static discharges
147 Tailplane tip lighting protector
148 CFC tailplane box structure
149 CFRP tailplane leading edge
150 Port tailplane integral fuel tank
151 All-moving tailplane pivot mounting
152 Tailplane sealing plates
153 Tailplane trim screw jack
154 Fin support structure
155 Cabin pressurisation valves (two)
156 Rear pressure bulkhead
157 Rear galley units
158 Wardrobe
159 Cabin rear entry door
160 Rear toilet compartments (four)
161 Rear cabin window panels
162 Bulk cargo hold door

163 Underfloor bulk cargo hold. cargo 11.3 m³ (400 ft³)
164 LD3 baggage containers (14 in rear hold)
165 Rear fuselage frame and stringer structure
166 Port mid-cabin door
167 CFRP wing root trailing edge fillet
168 Port inboard single-slotted flap segment
169 Main undercarriage support beam
170 Mainwheel leg pivot mounting
171 Hydraulic retraction jack
172 Inboard spoiler/lift dumper
173 Spoiler CFRP/honeycomb structure
174 Inboard flap track and carriage
175 Flap shroud ribs
176 Spoiler CFRP/honeycomb structure
177 Port five-segment outboard
178 Port outboard single-slotted flap

205 General Electric CF6-80E1A2 turbofan
206 Fan air (cold stream) exhaust duct
212 Engine pylon attachment point
213 Main undercarriage leg strut
213 Main undercarriage leg strut
214 Sidestay/breaker strut
215 Inner wing panel centre spar
216 Fuel pumps
217 Wing root bolted joint strap
218 Inboard integral fuel tank
219 Machined wing ribs
220 Bleed air supply duct to air conditioning system
221 Inboard leading edge slat segment
222 Pratt & Whitney PW4164 alternative powerplant (PW4174 in long-range version)

179 Flap track fairings
180 Fuel jettison
182 Aileron GFRP/honeycomb construction
188 Port navigation and strobe light
189 Wing tip fuel vent tank
190 Port leading edge slat segments
191 Slat de-icing air 'picolo' pipes
192 Telescopic air ducts
193 Slat guide rails
194 Slat guide rail fuel sealing 'cans'
195 Front spar
196 Wing rib construction
197 Lower wing skin/stringer panel with access manholes
198 Rear spar
199 Port wing integral fuel tank
200 De-icing air duct
201 Rolls-Royce Trent 768 alternative powerplant Trent 775 in long-range version
202 Port engine nacelle
203 Intake lip de-icing air duct
204 Engine fan casing

Mike Badrocke